IN SEARCH OF A FAITH MENTOR

IN SEARCH OF A FAITH MENTOR

The discovery will change the trajectory and quality of your life.

Ken McCray

KDC PUBLISHING

KDC Publishing
708.928.6143
www.deirdrelcunninghamenterprises.com/kdc-publishing

Ken L. McCray
929 Garfield Place
Danville, IL. 61832
217-274-8471

Unless otherwise indicated, Scripture quotations are taken from the
King James Version (KJV) – *public domain.*

Printed in the United States of America

Paperback ISBN-13: **979--8-9853206-0-2**

In Loving Memory of My Late Wife –

Renee Francine Hunt-McCray

- My Rock, My Greatest Fan, My Strongest Supporter and The Brightest Star,

We Miss You So Much!

DEDICATION

*The best man for my wedding was my friend, **Michael Rollins**. Although he has gone on to be with The Lord, he left an irrevocable imprint on my life. This writing is dedicated to him for his steadfast Faith, his example as a man of God, and his model as a man to men.*

*He was strength and wisdom to everyone, and possessed a genuine love for all. I still keep in touch with his son, **Michael Rollins Jr.**, and have asked him to write a dedication, which you are able to read below.*

A SPECIAL DEDICATION
From the Son about His Dad

My father, Michael Rollins, was one of the most dedicated individuals I have ever come across in my life. I watched in admiration as he worked 50-60 hours a week, 45 minutes away from home, was faithful to the ministry attending service numerous times per week, and was always studying the word of God in preparation for the church radio broadcast or for his opportunity to preach the word of God at our church.

His dedication to his family and his ministry made him great. But, his infectious smile and charming personality are what made you love him as a preacher, teacher, mentor & friend. Two major things about my father are 1) he was humble and 2) he was very approachable. Young or old could relate to and share with him. He spoke to you with respect and had the right words to encourage you; but yet, he always spoke the truth. This kept you coming back when you needed an ear, or sound advice, or just confirmation that you were doing the right thing.

He knew the scripture and could break it down in a way that all could comprehend. As a preacher, I considered him a teacher, it was rare that he "tuned up" per se. But, he always had a subject that related to popular culture or everyday life. In his everyday life, he loved to dress.

Whether it was his casual wear or his Sunday's best, he always put his best foot forward. He stayed current with fashion trends, which kept him in the loop with the younger generations. He spoke well to the younger population and inspired many.

I said all that to say this: those things made you want him around. You wanted to talk to him, confide in him, and gain his approval; not because he had titles, but because he lived by example. When you think of a mentor, it is a person that has been on the path you're looking to journey with the ability to communicate their insights to make you more effective in life. That person was my Dad.

by Michael Rollins Jr.

TABLE OF CONTENTS

FOREWORD

FOREWORD

by William E. Dickerson

This book is very readable and interesting, to say the least.

Author Ken McCray shares from his personal and candid perspective what he went through regarding connecting with a solid person who could mentor him. The enthusiasm with which Ken writes helps to draw one into the process of finding a faith mentor.

I met Ken McCray several years ago at a Leadership conference on the outskirts of Atlanta, Georgia, hosted by a mutual close friend. Since our initial meeting, we stayed in touch by phone calls and text messages.

I believe Ken is qualified to write on the subject of Faith. He has allowed himself to go through a journey of self-reflection.

As we meditate and reflect, we can ascertain what type of mentor we need in ministry and life. The author and I agree that faith cannot be monopolized by one denomination such as "The Word of Faith" movement; rather, faith is embraced based on our relationship with the Lord Jesus Christ.

Ken has a passion for leadership which exudes from him with basic conversations and writings. I believe he asked me to write the foreword to this book because I've been in many spaces wherein I have found good faith mentors. I also have been a good mentor to many over several years.

I am the founding pastor of an inner-city church in Boston, MA. What I found out amongst the majority of men within our church is that they need a solid mentor in their life. Therefore, I have been mentoring men in ministry for well over 30 years.

A great quote in this book was discovered through the writing wherein Galileo Galilei states, "You can never teach a man anything. You can only help him to discover what is in himself." Therefore, when one discovers a mentor, he or she discovers the person who can best pull out of them positive attributes which will help them to advance in life.

The scripture which seems to be the substratum for teaching on faith is found in Hebrews 11:1 – "Now faith is the substance of things hoped for and the evidence of things not seen."

To find a mentor who embraces faith on a level of attraction is not easy. However, it can be done when we are serious about our faith walk like Ken McCray.

If you are a person who appreciates a book that has also a workbook formatted style within its pages, then this is the book for you.

Let this book take you on a journey as you discover a faith mentor. Your willingness to mature in your relationship with Christ is based on faith principles that can cause you to be successful in life.

May the characters highlighted in this book move you to immerse yourself in practical and profound thinking on faith. Get ready to soar in ways that you thought were not attainable, for we know all things are possible through Jesus Christ.

Since faith, as the author puts it, "is the inner persuasion that something is true based on the word of God that causes us to act on what we believe," then get ready for corresponding actions.

As you read this book, the faith convictions of the author will grab you visually and viscerally as you confidently believe God for faith-filled success.

Rest assured, as you operate in faith, it's not wacky or weird; it's efficacious and beneficial.

Just as Elisha was the mentee to Elijah the mentor, let Ken McCray guide you through a process that is plain yet profound. Allow the Holy Spirit to open you up to the process of faith and spiritual maturation through faith mentorship.

The author's prayer of faith was the genesis of his quest to seek a faith mentor. Let the Lord lead and guide you on this powerful journey of faith discovery as well.

Foreword by
William E Dickerson II, MEd, MA, (Honorary) DD
Sr. Pastor and Prelate
Greater Love Tabernacle and Restoration Ministries
Boston, MA.

PREFACE

PREFACE

I did not see in my life the level of productivity that was possible. I was saved for over five years, I was dedicated, and I was Faithful to all my church assignments and responsibilities.

I read the Word of God, committed myself to memorize scripture, and fasted as prompted. However, I was not seeing the demonstration of spiritual productivity, for that matter, I did not know that powerful spiritual productivity, along with material prosperity, was even possible. Nor was I aware that Faith was the element that provided that productivity. The development of Faith to excel in the two aforementioned areas was not something that was a major subject or topic of conversation.

But, I was introduced to the teaching on Faith by

Dr. I.V. Hilliard. And, it was then I discovered that, as a believer, we can develop our Faith to be spiritually and materially productive.

This is when I began the journey of learning about Faith and how to develop Faith intentionally. I even realized that, at the point where I am now in my understanding of Faith and how it works, I am only scratching the surface.

However, in the process of growth in how to develop my Faith, I noticed that one of the things that are germane to the development of one's Faith is that of having a Faith *mentor* - a mentor who is living at the level and demonstrating the manifestation of productivity that the mentee desires to have.

A Faith mentor is one that is willing to share his or her experience and wisdom to assist the mentee in pulling out what is in them, and providing them with the insight to guide the mentee to the level, and above, where the mentor is living.

So, it is while having in mind this important piece in the Faith development process, coupled with my desire to see others maximize their life, that I have written this book. I intend that you the reader will glean from the principles contained in this writing and use them to elevate the quality of your life.

In a departure from my first two books - "A Brand Called Me" and "I've Fallen, But I Can Get Up" – this book's story format will intentionally capture your attention and only release it at the end.

At the conclusion, you will find this writing engaging and a very important piece of your Faith development process.

INTRODUCTION

INTRODUCTION

Mike Murdock, a prolific writer and millionaire, once stated "*Mentorship is the key to extraordinary success.*" This is a statement that rings true at all levels of life and has become a proven success principle time and time again.

What time has discovered about mentorship is that it has a threefold benefit. Mentoring will accelerate learning, develop raw and untapped abilities, and provide wisdom that enables one to avoid detours and many of life's pitfalls.

This principle involves the mentor taking their experience and learning that they have gained over time and then downloading it into the mentee.

Concerning mentorship, World Education Services states that "*...mentorship is a relationship* *between two people where the individual with more experience, knowledge, and connections can pass along what they have learned to a more junior individual within a certain field."*

Some businesses that are high performing businesses have incorporated mentorship in the culture of the business. They know and understand that mentorship is essential to high-level performance and the efficiency of the business. So, they are intentional with their mentorship program.

During my previous work time in two big-box retail stores, I served as an Assistant Manager and Recruiter, as well as what was called then a Regional Leadership Champion.

The founder of one of the big box retail stores was a drum major for mentoring, and he mandated that they have a mentorship program that was complete with a handbook. This handbook included exercises that were to be performed, timelines to be met, and accountability to the store manager to confirm assignments were completed. They approached the program with succession planning and development in mind.

One of the statements that I have heard about mentorship is this: *"You can never get out of a person what is not already in them."*

Galileo Galilei, the Italian natural philosopher, astronomer, and mathematician states, *"You cannot teach a man anything. You can only help him discover it within himself."* This means that the goal of mentorship is to bring the best out of the mentee.

It is to show them a more excellent way and help them to develop upward thinking, which is elevating and projecting thought to greater possibilities. It is to impart wisdom and guidance for great decision making, and great decision making is essential in life.

Why? Because the strongest and lasting impact on a person's life is found in the decisions they make. Decisions are the most powerful and longest-lasting, course-directing occurrence in a person's life, bar none.

That is why you hear, or you say, such statements as, "That was the best decision I could have made!" and "Increase your knowledge so that you can make an informed decision." and "Don't make a hasty decision," as well as "What logic was used to make that decision?"

Success Leaves Clues

In scripture, the writer of the wisdom book of Proverbs, King Solomon, was mentored by his father King David. As a result, Solomon knew what to ask for when God visited him in a dream and gave him carte blanche in prayer.

II Chronicles 1:

> *[7]In that night did God appear unto Solomon, and said unto him, "Ask what I shall give thee".*
>
> *[8]And Solomon said unto God, Thou hast shewed great mercy unto David my father, and hast made me to reign in his stead.*
>
> *[9]Now, **O LORD** God, let thy promise unto David my father be established: for thou hast made me king over a people like the dust of the earth in multitude.*
>
> *[10]Give me now wisdom and knowledge that I may go out and come in before this people: for who can judge this thy people that is so great?*
>
> *[11]And God said to Solomon, Because this was in thine heart, and thou hast not asked riches, wealth, or honour, nor the life of thine enemies, neither yet hast asked long life; but hast asked wisdom and knowledge for thyself, that thou mayest judge my people, over whom I have made thee king:*
>
> *[12] Wisdom and knowledge is granted unto thee; and I will give thee riches, and wealth, and honour, such as none of the kings have had that have been before thee, neither shall there any after thee have the like.*

But, this isn't the only instance of mentorship in the

Bible. You can find examples of mentorship demonstrated throughout scripture which communicate that the principle of mentorship is important. Some of those examples of mentorship are Moses for Joshua, Elijah for Elisha, and Naomi for Ruth.

With this importance in mind, apart from The Lord placing a mentor in your life, the initiative has to be taken to pursue a mentor. That pursuit involves identifying someone who has accomplished what you want to accomplish, doing successfully what you want to do, or living at the level of life you want to live.

Jim Rhone, bestselling author and world-renowned leadership trainer, states in his lectures: *"Success leaves clues."* The clues that he speaks of are in the successful person's character, behaviors, philosophy, practices, and mindsets; they are elements worth emulating.

The mentee identifies and duplicates them with their flavor to achieve the same level of success or higher.

That is what Solomon did: he duplicated his father's offering and expanded upon the prayer he heard his father prayer for him. He made it his own; and then, he expanded upon it to make it work for him. (See I Chronicles 29).

Just For Clarity

I am not saying a person cannot achieve success

without a mentor; but, I am saying emphatically that a mentor will accelerate and remove a great deal of the struggle out of the process.

In this book, two young men have realized that life has more to offer than what they are experiencing. They have noticed the difference the element of Faith has made in the lives of other credible people whereas they are living at a higher level and quality of life.

They discover that living at a higher level and quality of life occurred for those they observed as a result of them exercising the elements and principles of Faith.

This discovery prompts them to go on a search in pursuit of someone to mentor them in the area of Faith.

The end goal is to achieve an elevated life and a change in the quality of their life; not for vainglory, but for being more effective in life and to serve others.

In addition, it is because God said they could, according to Matthew 17:20b:

> [20b] *If ye have Faith as a grain of mustard seed, ye shall say unto this Mountain, Remove hence to yonder place; and it shall remove; and nothing shall be impossible unto you.*

The book picks up in the moment of the life of these two young men when their pursuit for a Faith Mentor is launched.

CHAPTER 1:

SOMETHING IS MISSING

IT is June, at the time of summer break. The day is sunny with a cool breeze. Zeteo, whose best friend and running partner is Calvin, is experiencing the frustration that will change his life forever.

Since Calvin is a close friend with whom he can express his frustrations, he calls Calvin up on the phone.
"Hey Calvin, what are you doing right now?"

" Why, what's going on?"

" I have a question for you. But, I want to come by and speak with you about it."

" Sounds good! Come on by. I will be downstairs in the basement doing some reading."

" Great! I will see you in about twenty minutes."

 Twenty minutes later, a knock comes on the door.

"Who is it?" asked Calvin's dad. "It's Zeteo the Leo, Mrs. Carter!"

" I got your *Leo!*" laughing, as she opens the door. "Calvin is downstairs in the basement."

"Thanks, Mrs. Carter!" as he hurries to the basement door and runs downstairs.

"Hey! What's up my friend?" asked Calvin, as they clasp hands and give each other the guy hug.

"Things are good, but not so good at the same time." says Zeteo.

"That sounds so contradictory." says Calvin. "Are you confused about something?"

"Yes, *things* are. Let me tell you what is confusing me." says Zeteo.

"Wait! Wait! Wait!" interrupts Calvin. "Let me share my confusion, which has become a frustration, with you first! Here it goes… I can't seem to get my life up to the level I want my life to be. It feels like I am just spinning my wheels! And, to make it worse, others around me are moving their life forward, it seems like, every month! I am not understanding the difference between me and them. I don't think they are smarter than me. They are not more gifted than me. But, they seem to be getting it done! Can you help me figure this out?"

Zeteo replied, "Calvin, I can identify with what you are feeling because I am wrestling with the same thing!"

"I am so perplexed by this that I am thinking about going to Ira Mountain." said Calvin.

"Ira Mountain?" asked Zeteo. "What is that, and where is it located?"

"I am reading this book that mentions Ira Mountain being the place to go to for answers to some of life's questions. A visit to Ira Mountain is the one thing everyone has in common who has an elevated life of quality, elevated character, a strong spiritual walk, and a visible increase in their life."

"Really?" asked Zeteo. "So, do they go and touch the Mountain? Bow at the Mountain? How does it happen for them?"

"Man, if it was only that simple!" laughed Calvin. "Besides, Zeteo, you know nothing worth accomplishing just unfolds into your lap! Worthwhile things are going to require effort and committed work."

"I know! I know!" Zeteo replied. "I am just desperate to see a change in my life's condition. As I look at the quality of my life, I am struggling on multiple levels – spiritual, emotional and financial. Now, my life is not trash; that is not what I am saying. I just know there is something better, and I want better. However, I feel like I am missing what I need to have to get it to that better."

Calvin replies, "I can relate to how you feel. It is like better is inside, but you are unclear as to how to pull it out."

"Yeah! Yeah! That's it!" exclaimed Zeteo. "That's it! I know that I have accepted Jesus as The Christ and Son of God, and I have confessed Him as my personal Savior. I am born again and I love God. I love the anointing and I am Faithful to church. But, it appears that is the foundation upon which we are to build, and that there is more available. I keep hearing the mention of the word Faith and being developed in Faith by so many that are successful and experiencing a higher quality of life. It sounds like they operate Faith to receive and experience significant results in life. I know we all have received the *measure* of Faith; but, I have little understanding of it or how to operate it. This is where I need direction."

"I know! I know!" says Calvin.

"I am ready to put the work in!" Zeteo exclaims. "Okay, so what does the book say to do once you get to the Ira Mountain?"

"In the book, it says, upon arriving at the north side of Ira Mountain, locate the winding road leading up the Mountain."

"That sounds easy!" said Zeteo. "Where does it lead to?"

"The book said it would lead to a person who has lived in that Mountain forever; and that he never comes down. He just waits for people to come to him. The book calls him 'Nootropic'."

"Forever?! Come on now!" says Zeteo.

"I am just stating what the book says, so don't crucify the messenger!" They both chuckle.

"Besides!" says Calvin, "the best way to prove it out is to go to the Mountain and see for ourselves. However, there are two things the book pointed out that we must watch for. *First*, there are going to be two roads: one leads up the Mountain, the other leads in a circle around the Mountain. However, the book does say there is a way to discern which road is which once you see them. *Second*, Nootropic is particular about who he receives: he receives a person based on hunger and determination; and if those two factors are not at the level he wants, then he declines to speak with you."

"That is interesting." replied Zeteo.

"Why?" asked Calvin.

"Because it means that those who made it to Ira Mountain and discerned the correct road leading up met Nootropic. But, not all had a hunger and determination at the level he was looking for; so, he sent them back down the mountain." Zeteo paused and said, "I find great encouragement in this!"

"Again, what do you mean?" says Calvin.

"First, we are not going to be sent back down the mountain. Second, since others have met him, and he received them, and afterward, they demonstrated a change in the quality of their life, it means it has been duplicated several times over.

This proves it can be repeated by others as well, namely me!"

"Well, don't leave me out!" replied Calvin.

"Of course not!" chuckled Zeteo.

"So, how do we get to this Ira Mountain? I am looking forward to meeting this Nootropic person!"

"According to the book, the directions state to go inside the forest park, identify the north direction, then keep walking in that direction."

"For how far?" asked Zeteo.

"It does not say."

"Well, what should we look for to know we are getting close?" asked Zeteo.

"It does not state anything about what to look for."

"Well, how long will it take?" asked Zeteo.

"It does not state how long it will take to get there either."

Being visibly frustrated, Zeteo says, "Well, I guess we must trust we will come to the Ira Mountain before we run out of sunlight or walk up on something we don't want to encounter."

"Yep! Sounds like a trust walk to me, as well as a mind to do what it takes to get there! Good thing tomorrow is Saturday, since it sounds like it is going to be an all-day affair."

"Then, so be it! Let's meet early in the morning, around 5 am!" "Whoa! 5 am?" Calvin exclaims. "I am not normally out of bed until 8:30 am on a Saturday!"

"Yes sir!" replies Zeteo. "If you want something different, you must do something different. *I place great value on this change; and, that which you place the greatest value, for that you will make the greatest sacrifice.*"

"Well, when you put it like that, I must check myself and assess if I have placed great value on my change." He pauses for a moment, then says, "So, 5 am it is!"

They shake hands and give each other another guy hug. Then, Zeteo runs up the stairs and speaks to Mr. and Mrs. Carter on his way out the front door.

CHAPTER 2:

LET THE SEARCH BEGIN

Zeteo can hardly sleep due to his anticipation level. He is up and calling Calvin at 4:30 am!

"Calvin, are you awake?"

"Yes! I could hardly sleep. I will meet you in the forest. And, bring your compass!"

So, they meet at the forest entrance and set the compass to due North. As they travel North, true to the book, they come to two roads.

"They both look the same!" says Calvin, in a confused tone. "The only difference is one has more footprints than the other. Since there are more footprints on this one, let's take this one."

Zeteo speaks up, "Hold on! Let's think this through first. The one with the most footprints means it is the popular road. But, the one that is least traveled indicates that few are traveling on this one. So, let's take the one with the fewest footprints."

They agreed and took the road least traveled; and it turns out to be the one that leads *up* the mountain, instead of the one that leads around the mountain.

After an extended time, they wanted to quit and go back down the mountain; but, they fought the temptation, reassured each other they were fully committed and agreed they had come too far to turn back at this point.

They finally make it to the top of Ira Mountain. And there, sitting on a rock, is a very commonly dressed man. He has no motion or activity but seems to respond to their presence.

Calvin speaks up and says, "Excuse me, sir. We are looking for Mr. Nootropic."

He responds saying, "I am he. And I know what you seek."

Calvin, with a question mark in his voice, says, "You do?"

"Few have sought me out before you, and I rewarded them abundantly. They spend the time with me to receive what they need for their journey, and to secure the answers to questions that would bring change to their lives. It is my rule, however, to never spend time with anyone who does not have the determination to change. This determination to change burns so hotly inside that no barrier, obstacle or roadblock will deter them. So hot that no critic, naysayer, nor skeptic will be able to talk them out of what they pursue. So hot that they will stick with the process no matter what circumstances or situations try to defy them.

So hot that length of time will not outlast their patience. Until you are at that level of hot, it is not worth the investment of my time."

"Mr. Nootropic, we are determined in all the ways you just said. Please tell us what you would like for us to do."

"Okay. Since your will is set with a no-quit mindset, I will feed that determination and arm you with the tools for change. I will provide you with information to feed the hunger of your determination, and you in turn will aim your determination toward goals. But you will need to go back home and examine your heart and discern whether it is conducive for the growth of faith and big ideas. Without this understanding and condition of heart, you will not be able to produce the change needed to move your life to the next level. Come back tomorrow, and I will provide you with a key that will link to the understanding I just mentioned; and, it will become the key to your life from here on."

They both respond with great excitement, "Sure we will! Is there anything else you would like for us to do in preparation for tomorrow?"

Mr. Nootropic looks intently into their eyes and states, "Now, faith is the substance of things hoped for, and the evidence of things not seen. I would like for you both to memorize and meditate on this verse overnight, and take notes on your thoughts. **a**) What is the essence of it, and **b**) can you embrace the fact that this verse is a defining factor of anyone's life? When you grasp this truth, it will begin to govern and guide your life. This verse describes how everyone functions, whether intentional or unintentional. It is either working for their life for a higher quality of life, or they are working it against themselves in a negative way. The difference is how the principle is used because we all use it. Here are a few other questions I would like for you to consider: **c**) How much of your mind and thoughts do you control, and **d**) how much of your mind are you working and focusing on a project?"

With these things in mind, Calvin and Zeteo trudged back down the Mountain, not aware of how long they had been gone.

Once they reached the bottom, exhausted and tired, they said one to the other "I have thought up an appetite! Where would you like to eat? said Calvin.

Zeteo answered with determination in his voice, "I am not sure where we are going to eat, but I am going to go home first and locate a pen and notebook; then, go to work on the assignment that he charged us with."

Calvin responded with an affirmative, "Man, that was what I was thinking also!"

"Then let's go home, get freshened up, grab paper and pen, and meet at McCray's Barbeque place in an hour."

"Sounds like a winner to me! I will meet you there in about one hour. What time is it now?"

"7:00 pm." Zeteo answered.

"Okay, then I will see you at 8:00 pm."

On the way home, Zeteo pondered the questions that he and Calvin were challenged with. He reflected on the word *Faith* and wondered if he could gain a greater understanding of the word.

"Since, according to Mr. Nootropic, it is the substance of things hoped for and the evidence of things not seen, it appears to be something that I need to understand." as he thought along the way.

He remembered a lesson he received concerning the application of any principle. The lesson revealed this principle:

> To enhance the application of a principle, there must be a level of understanding of the function and meaning of the word or phrase.

He also remembered that he could not confuse the definition of a word with the operation that the word conveys. It is the difference between memorizing a word and working on that word.

Zeteo thought within himself, "I want to see results from my Faith – Faith fruit – the things hoped for and the manifestation of things not seen. So," he said to himself, "I will make Understanding Faith my goal and the top priority for the next three months."

Upon arriving home, his mom and dad asked him where he had been.

Zeteo answered, "I have been to the Mountain top."

His dad laughed and replied, "Ok, Martin." Then his dad asked, "So, what was the trip to the Mountain all about?"

Zeteo answered, "Dad, to be honest with you, I did not know the trip was going to be made until last night. I was only trying to discover how to take my life to the next level, which began with studying and looking at successful people and realizing that they know something I don't know."

Zeteo's father asked, "How did you come to that conclusion?"

Zeteo replied, "Because they have a quality of life I don't have; not that I am envying them. It is just that, if they have the mission and model, along with the character, confidence, and content, and it is working for them; then, to get that quality, I will need to adopt and mirror their actions. All that they have is available to anyone who will go after it. So, I am going to start gleaning from what they know because I want it in my life. I don't want *their* stuff…I want my own. I pulled Calvin into this with me. Our search brought us to Ira Mountain to meet a guy named Mr. Nootropic, and he challenged us in few areas:

➢ *first*, understanding Faith and how it operates.
➢ *second,* work on my mind, thoughts, patterns,

beliefs, and behaviors to become everything I need to become to have what I want.

Once I grasp these two things, it will assist me in the release of the potential that is inside of me.

Zeteo's dad replied, "Hmm, I have heard of him! Mr. Nootropic is a wise man. Well, son, it appears that you are in search of a *Faith Mentor*."

"You know what dad? I believe you are correct in saying that. I am going to freshen up and go meet Calvin at McCray's Barbeque."

REFLECTION 1

RELFECTION 1

What are your take-aways so far?

1. _____

_____

_____

_____

2. _____

_____

_____

_____

3. _____

_____

_____

_____

Do you see anything that may be missing from your Faith development process that you can begin to implement?

_____

_____

_____

_____

_____

_____

Is there anything that you will begin to do differently?

1. _____

_____

_____

_____

2. _____

_____

_____

_____

3. _____

_____

_____

_____

CHAPTER 3:

THE SEARCH INTENSIFIES

After freshening up, Zeteo runs out the door, and on his way, calls Calvin and asks him to be ready to google the word "Faith" in the Bible.

Thought: *The drive to dig and discover is essential to the forward movement of one's life. However, that drive must have a direction to produce effective for movement. It is like setting goals and intentional outcomes: Goals produce direction and are necessary for you to know where you are going. Intentional outcomes verify being on target.*

Upon getting off the phone, Calvin goes directly to his laptop and begins to feverously plug in the query for the mention of the word "Faith" in the Bible. In the process of the research, Calvin makes a few interesting discoveries.

He closes up the laptop, gathers up his things, and rushes out the door to meet Zeteo at McCray's Barbeque.

Calvin arrives at McCray's Barbeque within twenty minutes; but, Zeteo was already there waiting on him.. Calvin could hardly put his things down on the table before he began sharing his findings.

"My friend, listen to what I have found out!"

"Come on with it!" says Zeteo.

"Okay, here it is. There are a total of 21,145 verses in the Old Testament, and the words *Faith* and *Believe* are mentioned a total of 21 times. There are a total of 7,957 verses in the New Testament and the words *Faith* and *Believe* are mentioned 369 times. There is a strong emphasis on *Belief* and *Faith* found in scripture, and neither one belongs to any movement or denomination; such as what is called The Word of Faith Movement. The matter of Faith is personal, not a movement or denomination. To look a little more specific to the weight that is placed on the words *Faith* and *Believe* in light of our Christian experience, this quick research has given me a clearer understanding of what God says about them. I looked at the definitions and biblical scenarios around the exercising of *Belief* and *Faith*. Would you like for me to share what I discovered?"

Zeteo replied, "Come on with it…I am on the edge of my seat!"

Calvin continues, "There is a threefold cord which consists of *Hope*, *Believe*, and *Faith*. Now, when we look at hope, there must be a differentiation made between natural/physical hope and biblical hope.

"So what is the difference?" Zeteo asked.

"Okay, here is the difference: Natural/physical hope encompasses wishing, uncertainty, question, and wondering if it will occur. But, Biblical hope is *the earnest expectation of the desired outcome, of which outcome is based on the promises of The Word of God and The Voice of God.*

"Then what does it mean to *Believe*?" asked Zeteo.

"Good question, my friend! Here is what I discovered believe means: It is an act of my will to accept something as a fact or truth even though there is no sense realm evidence. And note the aspect that states, 'It is an act of the will.' That means that it is a conscious choice that is within my control. This addresses what Mr. Nootropic meant by the challenge: 'How much of your mind and thoughts do you control, and how much of your mind is working and focusing on a project? '"

Zeteo in a super excited voice replied, "Wow! I can see what you are saying! I must exercise biblical hope, and I must place credibility on The Promises in The Word of God and on the Character of God to decide as an act of my will to accept His Word and His Voice as fact and truth. Okay, so now I am hyped up! What else did you discover about *Faith*?"

Calvin can hardly keep his seat. "My friend, this is what I have come to understand about *Faith*, and it is exciting! First, it is not outward in any respect; it is an inner persuasion. Second, it always carries with it a corresponding action. With both of these things in mind, here is what I discovered about *Faith*: Faith is the inner persuasion that something is true or factual, based on The Word of God that causes you to act on what you

believe. That inner persuasion is an inward picture drawn and framed by The Word of God that is so clear, so strong, and so real that it affects the way you speak,
think, and behave and makes you uncomfortable when you are not living inside of it."

"I get it!" Zeteo exclaimed. "*Faith is my Word of God reality! Faith animates and brings solidness to what I am biblically hoping for and have willingly decided and chosen to accept as truth.* Wow! There goes that threefold cord you mentioned. So I will have to meditate on this...Hey Calvin!"

"What?" Calvin responded.

Zeteo says with intensity in his voice, "Here is what I just realized: My thinking, conversation, behavior, and the way I am believing will reveal when I am in Faith and when I am not."

"That is so true, Zeteo!" says Calvin with a bit of relief in his voice that he and Zeteo are on the same thought path. "Boy! Mr. Nootropic is going to be impressed with this insight."

"Well, I am going to chew on this discussion...and on this burger and fries I am getting ready to order!" said Zeteo as he chomps down on his burger.

They both laugh!

CHAPTER 4:

THE FOLLOW-UP – *FAITH FREQUENCY*

The next day after church, Zeteo and Calvin met at Ira Mountain. They located the path and travelled up to see Mr. Nootropic.

To their surprise, Mr. Nootropic was waiting on them and shocked them with an unexpected statement: "Some do not return." He went on to say, "But, I have been looking forward to *your* return."

Zeteo and Calvin looked at each other dumbfounded for a moment, but regained their composure and asked, "What caused you to expect us to return?"

Mr. Nootropic responded, "There is a hunger that can be seen in both of you. Furthermore, there is a drive that can be sensed when you come in contact with someone determined to bring a new direction to their life. There is a certain presence and fire in their eyes." he stated as he looking into their eyes. "Please come into my home and have a seat with me at the table. I can share a few things with you to bring clarity to building your Faith." As they take their seats at the kitchen table, Mr. Nootropic makes a statement that grabs their attention immediately, "There is what I will call a *Frequency* of Faith."

"A *frequency*?!" blurted out Zeteo?

"Yes, a *Frequency*. But, it is *spiritual* frequency."

"Mr. Nootropic, would you provide us with something that can help us understand this concept?" asked Calvin

Mr. Nootropic in a seemingly anxious posture because of the boys' determination to understand, replied, "Sure! Let's use Acts 14:9 as a spiritual example and then bring in an application of it in the natural.

> **The same heard Paul speak who steadfastly beholding him, and perceiving that he had Faith to be healed.** [Acts 14:9]

He leans in toward the boys and continues, "My *Faith Seekers*, that is an example of Frequency. Apostle Paul was not necessarily going by physical indications. He perceived, which means *to become aware of something cognitively or by an intangible means*. This is what is called *spiritual material*. *Spiritual Frequency* requires tuning into the spiritual transmission of a thing that is occurring at the time. In the natural, it occurs with radio and television, which operates on *reoccurring vibrations that become waves*. Scientists discovered that it occurs in electromagnetic fields. *An Electromagnetic Field is a combination of invisible, electric, and magnetic areas of force.*

"Electromagnetic Fields??" chuckled Calvin. "That seems a little far removed from Faith-building."

Mr. Nootropic quickly responds, "Not at all! Because, for

every natural law - law meaning an established governing principle of operation that consistently occurs and produces the same results all the time – there is a parallel, spiritual law that produces consistent results all the time. The scripture states in 1 Corinthians 15:46

> *Howbeit that was not first which is spiritual, but that which is natural; and afterward that which is spiritual.*[1 Corinthians 15:46]

And, just like the law of electricity was discovered, understood, controlled, and intentionally used to produce light consistently, so it is with the law of Faith.

Mr. Nootropic continues, *"Where is boasting then? It is excluded. By what law? Of works? Nay: but by the law of Faith.* [Romans 3:2] Once the *Law* of Faith is discovered, understood, controlled, and intentionally used, it will produce consistent results." He pauses and asks, "Are you still with me?"

"Yes Sir!" they both say excitedly.

"Good!" said Mr. Nootropic.   "Now, in the definition of Electromagnetic Fields - *a combination of invisible, electric, and magnetic fields of force* – there are three words that speak to Faith: Invisible, Magnetic, and Force; all of which operate within the *Law* of Faith. Faith is *invisible* but perceivable. Faith is *magnetic*: it draws things. Faith is a *force* that causes things to happen. When we operate by the *Law* of Faith – *For we walk by Faith, not by sight.* [2 Corinthians 5:7] – then the *invisible, magnetic force* of Faith produces manifestation. However, just like radio and television frequencies, the dial must be set on the correct vibration or channel.

Zeteo says with great excitement, "I think I get it! When I think about radio stations such as FM and AM, the FM normally has a stronger frequency and greater range than the AM. And, the connection for receiving requires various levels of strength."

Calvin, with the same excitement in his voice as Zeteo, says, "Now I see why Jesus said in scripture *Why are ye fearful, O ye of little Faith?* (Matthew 8:26), and in various other texts stated things like *...And being not weak in Faith, he considered not his own body now dead* (Romans 4:19), *...Verily I say unto you, I have not found so great Faith, no, not in Israel* (Matthew 8:10), and *because that your Faith groweth exceedingly* (2 Thessalonians 1:3). All of these represent the strength and spiritual range of their Faith."

Mr. Nootropic commends Calvin for gaining that understanding, and continues to share, "Now, a Faith Seeker must go to work to deliberately and intentionally grow and build their Faith. The reason is simple: Faith Frequency needs to connect to the element and channel of The Kingdom of God to receive from God."

"Wow!" Zeteo and Calvin say at the same time, as they look wide-eyed at each other. Then, they say to each other, "Are you thinking what I am thinking?"

"Yes!" as they state in unison. "Romans 10:17 and 2 Corinthians 4:13"

Calvin quotes, "***So then Faith cometh by hearing – tuned in frequency – and hearing by the Word of God****!* [Romans 10:17]"

Zeteo anxiously chimes in quoting the second scripture, "We had the same spirit – waves of Faith, according to ***as it is written, I believed, therefore have I spoken; we also believe, and therefore speak****!* [2 Corinthians 4:13]"

Calvin chimes in again, "So then, as a way of processing this aspect of the operation of Faith for connecting with and *receiving* The Goodness of God, Psalms 65:4 states ***Blessed is the man whom thou choosest, and causest to approach unto Thee, that he may dwell in Thy courts: We Shall be Satisfied with The Goodness of Thy House, (storehouse) even of Thy Holy Temple****.*"

Zeteo then continues, "Therefore, I can look at it this way: Favor has a Faith Frequency, according to Psalm 5:12. The Blessings has a Faith Frequency, according to Proverbs 10:22. The Word of Truth has a Faith Frequency, according to John 8:31-32. The Truth of The Promises has a Faith Frequency, according to Galatians 3:13-14. And, Hope has a Faith Frequency, according to Hebrews 11:1. WOW! So then, we have to be *dialed in* with our Faith – confident believing – so that it becomes a strong inner Faith Frequency that receives!"

Mr. Nootropic replies, "This is correct! This *inner* Faith Frequency must become an inner picture that is so clear, so strong, so real, so intense, and so sincere that it produces in you a persuasion so powerful until it allows you to see yourself in possession of your _it_ for which you will not be denied.

"YEEES!" exclaim Calvin and Zeteo.

Mr. Nootropic continues, "Consider Mark 9:23 ***Jesus said unto him if thou canst believe, all things are possible to him that believeth.*** A strong, level Faith Frequency says 'I own it.'"

Mr. Nootropic rising from the table says, "With that being said, the day is far spent. It is time for you to take what we have covered and meditate on it, asking God how to expand upon it."

"Now, I don't want to leave because this is so good!" said Zeteo as he gets up from the table. "But, we look forward to coming back soon to share our findings and receive additional insight and revelation on the Frequency of Faith and how to operate in it."

Mr. Nootropic reaches and gets a paper that was on the table. "I have prepared something for you that you are to study and review often. Once it is in your spirit, it will be a governing principle of your life."

Calvin received the paper and put it away in his notebook, but didn't look at what was on it.

They gathered their things and left, almost skipping back down the Mountain for the joy of the teaching of the Word of Faith.

CHAPTER 5:

CHANNELS OF FAITH

Once they made it to the bottom of Ira Mountain, Zeteo says to Calvin, "So, let me see what is on the paper."

"Okay." said Calvin. He removed the paper from his notebook and opened it up. "Wow! It is the explanations and examples of the items we covered in our discussion with Mr. Nootropic just now."

"Let me see! Let me see!" says Zeteo. "The paper has <u>*Channels* of Faith</u> to lock our Faith Frequency into. <u>Channel 1</u> is <u>The Person of God</u> – believe God. Genesis 15:6 *And he believed in The Lord; and He counted it to him for righteousness. A righteousness that is received by Faith in God.* Romans 4:21-25 *And being fully persuaded that, what He had promised, he was able also to perform. And therefore it was imputed to him for righteousness. Now it was not written for his sake alone, that it was imputed to him; But for us also, to whom it shall be imputed, if we believe on him that raised up Jesus our Lord from the dead; Who was delivered for our offenses, and was raised again for our justification.*"

Zeteo continues, "<u>Channel 2</u> is <u>The Name of Jesus</u> – an intimate relationship with the name of Jesus until it becomes our own. Acts 3:6 – *silver & gold have I none, but such as I have, give I unto you in the name of Jesus of Nazareth.*" Zeteo pauses and looks in the distance with his finger on his chin, "Do I have the level of intimacy with Him – Jesus – that I can say His name is mine in ownership?" Then, he looks at Calvin and says, "When we say His name, we know that there is something about His name – authority, position, accomplishment – that gives us confidence in the legal right to exercise His Name for reigning and governorship."

Calvin picks up reading from the paper Mr. Nootropic gave them, "And, Channel 3 is The Word of God – this requires an intimate relationship with the word of God, which will *release* what is in His word to produce a manifestation of Faith in our life."

Then Zeteo affirms, "How do we *get* this manifested result? It *must* become what you operate in and live by. It *must* become your code of conduct. Matthew 7:22-23 is a reference to an intimate relationship with His name, with *God*, and with His Word."

Defining Believing

Calvin continues, "Faith is a medium of exchange. It is the heart of God, and Faith *is* God. Romans 14:23 states, *...whatsoever is not of Faith is sin.* Therefore, the question arises, does Faith have a character? The answer is Yes! Faith is a spirit and has character, according to 2 Corinthians 4:13 *We having the same spirit of Faith, according as it is written, I believed, and therefore have*

I spoken; we also believe, and therefore speak; Romans
10:17 *So then Faith cometh by hearing, and hearing by
the word of God.* and John 6:63 *It is the spirit that
quickeneth; the flesh profiteth nothing: the words that I
speak unto you, they are spirit, and they are life."*

"WHEW!" exclaims Zeteo.

"I know right!" replies Calvin. "Faith has character – spirit
– and the aim is to incorporate the character of Faith –
confident trust and reliance on God – in our life."

Zeteo responds, "I see. We have to measure where we are
with this question: How much of the character of Faith,
level of confident trust and reliance is in our life?
Nowhere, for the most part; at least, to the degree that it is
perceivable"

"Yes!" says Calvin. "We must move past a surface level of
Faith and expectation to experience the demonstration,
manifestation, and deep moves of God."

"What will be one of the measurements regarding the
strength of the spirit and character of Faith within us?" asks
Zeteo.

"The main thing is, when our heart does not believe it and
our mouth does not say it, and there is noise in our mind,
these things will block the spirit of Faith and prevent the
formulation of the character of Faith in us. Therefore, one
measurement will be the substance of what we say."

As soon as that last word was read, Sarkikós, one of their

friends on the young-adult basketball team, dribbled up to them and asked, "Hey there! Where have you guys been? The team has missed you! We could have used those 3-point shots yesterday that you fellas bring to the game."

"How did the game go?" asked Calvin.

"We ended up losing by 3 points." Sarkikós replied.

"You should have put that *Magic Johnson* defense on 'em!" replied Zeteo in jest while laughing.

To which Calvin replies, "You know his defense is broke!" as they all chuckle.

"Well, it is good enough to shut *you* down, Calvin!" as he waves Calvin off with laughter. "But seriously, when are you and Zeteo coming back to the team?"

"It may be a while before we get back because right now we are working on a Faith project." answers Calvin.

"*Faith project*?! **W**hat does *that* mean?" exclaimed Sarkikós.

"It means we are working on growing our Faith on purpose so that we can change the quality of our life." replied Zeteo.

"That Faith stuff does not work!" scoffs Sarkikós, "I tried it for a couple of days and I saw no difference."

"That is because you tried it and never made a commitment to the process." Zeteo said emphatically.

"I need to see something to prove it works. And, right now, neither of you is showing any improvement in the quality of your life. So, I am going to go and work it out on the court, and I will check the *Faith Boys* out on the rebound. Get it: rebound, and playing basketball?" Sarkikós says sarcastically while chuckling.

"That was corny, Sarkikós."

Laughing, Sarkikós dribbles off into the sunset.

Facts Analysis

Zeteo looks at Calvin and says, "You know, there is some truth to what he said."

"What do you mean?" Calvin asked

"Well, when we live by Faith, there ought to be some fruit and change that should be shown." Zeteo said.

"You know, that does seem to make sense. Let's do something: let's mark where we are now and track our progress." says Calvin.

"Yeah!" exclaims Zeteo.

"What we need is a journal-like product where we can write down what we have as our Faith goals and where we are spiritually, personally, and materially at the moment, and where we believe to be over a defined period. We will watch for changes and manifestation, and note them as we go. Here, let me draw something up."

Calvin quickly sketches on his paper a diagram (on the next page). "Take a look. What do you think?"

"I like it! This is nice." Zeteo said with great enthusiasm.

"So, let's work it." they both say, as they give each other a high five.

(Note: The diagram the boys drew is on the following page. Feel free to utilize this tool for your own Faith Journey.)

This is the diagram drawn by Calvin and Zeteo.

Date: _____

aith Principle Exercised:	**Faith Goals** Spiritual:	Challenges that occurred:
_____		
_____	Family:	
_____		
_____	Financial:	
_____		How was it overcome:
_____	Physical:	
_____	Material:	
_____		
_____	Time spent studying Faith:	Faith scripture memorized :
aith Principles Learned:		

REFLECTION 2

REFLECTION 2

What are your take-aways to this point?

1. _____
_____
_____
_____

2. _____
_____
_____
_____

3. _____
_____
_____
_____

Do you see anything that may be missing from your Faith development process that you can begin to implement?

_____
_____
_____
_____
_____
_____
_____
_____
_____

Is there anything that you will begin to do differently?

1. _____
   _____
   _____
   _____

2. _____
   _____
   _____
   _____

3. _____
   _____
   _____
   _____

CHAPTER 6:

FAITH CRITERION

"Hey Calvin! There is something on the back of the paper that Mr. Nootropic gave you, and it looks like definitions."

Calvin, with eyes bucked, "Yes, it sure is! These are going to be very helpful. But, before we get too excited, we have to ask ourselves a question. And that is, how are we going to approach these definitions?"

"What do you mean, *how are we going to approach these definitions?*" exclaimed Zeteo. "We are going to memorize them. Duh!"

With his eyes squinted and his forehead wrinkled, Calvin replies, "I learned a truth some time ago that has been an asset ever since. The truth is this: You don't just memorize a definition only; but you have to internalize what you memorize. When you internalize what you memorize, that which is internalized is positioned to both grow you and guide you. In principle, that is what David was saying when he stated in Psalm 119:11

> **Thy word have I hid in mine heart, that I might not sin against thee.**

It is also addressed by Jesus when He states in Luke 6:45

*A good man out of the good treasure of his
heart bringeth forth that which is good; and an
evil man out of the evil treasure of his heart
bringeth forth that which is evil: for of the
abundance of the heart his mouth speaketh.*

It is internalized when it becomes your reality and it is
practiced to the degree that it becomes your behavior, your
attitude, and your life philosophy. These definitions that
come from Ira Mountain are rules of life, as well as
principles of life to live by."

"Whoa! Calvin, I get it! Thanks so much for the insight."
says Zeteo while patting Calvin on the back. "From now
on, I am going to approach memorization differently. I
mean, if I want to see a change in my life, this is going to
be one good way to accomplish that change." as he gives a
thumbs up to Calvin. "Okay, let's look at these
definitions... Oops! I mean, let's look at these *life
principles*."

Calvin chuckles and says, "That's it, my friend! Way to
adjust. Because you can't expect to get different results
when there is no behavior change."

"Do you know what we should do, Calvin? We should also
do some more research on Faith and its meaning,
mechanics, and how it operates."

"Super! Let's burn the midnight oil and dig out the
principles and nuggets." Calvin replies excitedly.

"Done. Let's go to work on it! Start small, but dream
big!" said Zeteo.

Calvin replies, "But first, let's meditate on these definitions that Mr. Nootropic gave us."

Zeteo agrees, "Okay, let's take a look!"

- **Believe:** the act of one's will to accept as truth, without any sense realm evidence.
- **Faith:** inner persuasion that something is true based on The Word of God, even though you do not have any sense realm evidence, but is strong and clear enough, and so real that it causes you to act on what you believe
- **Faith Operation**: the spiritual principle that taps into the creative power of God made available to man whereby he/she can transform his/her situation, condition, or circumstances in the natural that God has given man dominion over
- **Faith Confirmation:** the Word of God drawing an inner picture so real, so clear and so strong that it becomes uncomfortable to live outside the frame of that inner picture.
- **Faith Action:** corresponding behavior and conduct in agreement and aligned with what you believe
- **Faith Confession:** to make a statement in agreement with The Word of God; it is a choice, which is not the denial of what is appearing, but it is making a decision to say what God says and not what appears; pulling into reality what The Word of God says to drive out what appears
- **Faith Attitude:** a state of mind and disposition taken about believing; a state of being that is

resolved as the way of life."

"Wow, Calvin, I am getting it!" said Zeteo in amazement. "The process of gaining an understanding of all these seven terms, and becoming skillful in their application, is what moves one's personal life and effective ministry forward. However, to accomplish either one of these, understanding or skillfulness in the elements of Faith, requires one to be diligent in the study of the topic of Faith."

"I see something here." said Calvin. "These seven terms, with their definitions, need to be clarified and need elaboration regarding their application."

"Yeah." Zeteo consented. "It also appears that they must be performed in their proper sequence."

Calvin continued, "This, I feel, is vital to the process of receiving and seeing the demonstration that the Godkind of Faith is designed to produce as presented in Mark 11:22-25."

"Exactly. I would likewise say that these seven terms with their definitions are like components of the *Law* of Faith which is mentioned in Romans 3:27. And these seven terms together equal how Faith operates." Zeteo stated confidently.

"So then, these terms are Principles and Rules that govern Faith, and are essential and necessary to our understanding of how Faith operates. They are also essential to learning how to operate by them to get the desired results. Once we know and understand the operation of the Law of Faith, with the rules and principles that govern The Law of Faith, we won't hit and miss, but we can come into Faith on purpose." Calvin explained.

"Man, when *this* happens, there will be no guesswork, and our confidence will be stronger!"

"Exactly, as you say!" said Calvin, and they both chuckle as he continues. "We will have strong confidence when we exercise the Word of God. We will have *confident expectation* because the law of Faith does not contain a clause for doubt or hesitation; and there is no room for begging."

Zeteo jumps in, "When we know we are operating in Faith, we become bold – yes, it instills boldness. Additionally, when we know the principles, rules, and laws that govern Faith, we can always measure where our Faith is by those criteria."

"Yep. So, now we need to outline that criterion." Calvin stated.

On another sheet of paper they wrote the following:

CRITERIA

Hebrews 11:1-6 (KJV)

[1]Now Faith is the substance of things hoped for, the evidence of things not seen. [2]For by it the elders obtained a good report. [3]Through Faith we understand that the worlds were framed by the word of God so that things which are seen

were not made of things which do appear. [4]By Faith Abel offered unto God a more excellent sacrifice than Cain, by which he obtained witness that he was righteous, God testifying of his gifts: and by it he being dead yet speaketh. [5]By Faith Enoch was translated that he should not see death; and was not found, because God had translated him: for before his translation he had this testimony, that he pleased God. [6]But without Faith it is impossible to please him: for he that cometh to God must believe that he is, and that he is a rewarder of them that diligently seek him.

Mark 9:23 (KJV)
[23]Jesus said unto him, If thou canst believe, all things are possible to him that believeth.

Habakkuk 2:4 (KJV)
[4]Behold, his soul which is lifted up is not upright in him: but the just shall live by his Faith.

1 John 5:4 (KJV)
[4]For whatsoever is born of God overcometh the world: and this is the victory that overcometh the world, even our Faith.

Galatians 3:5 (KJV)
[5]He therefore that ministereth to you the Spirit, and worketh miracles among you, doeth he it by the works of the law, or by the hearing of Faith?

Calvin declared, "Because of these verses, it can be concluded that there can never be too much emphasis on the subject of Faith."

"E-Xactly!" replied Zeteo, as they both chuckle.

CHAPTER 7:

FAITH EXPLAINED

Around this time, their pastor comes around the corner on her daily walk.

"Hey Pastor Thomas!" said Zeteo. How is it going?" as they both try to keep up with her pace.

"Just fine, young men. How are you both, and what are you two up to right now? Staying out of trouble, right!" as she chuckles.

"You know us, Pastor T., we are *good*!"

"Yes, I *do* know you both, and that is why I was confirming that you are staying out of trouble." as they all laughed.

"Pastor T., can you help us out?" said Zeteo.

"We are diving into the subject of Faith; not just to accumulate a lot of head knowledge about the subject, but to work Faith in our life so that we can see some change in the quality of our life. You may even say that we are *In Search of a Faith Mentor*." Calvin explained.

"That is a noble pursuit there, young men. Tell you what: I will be through with my workout and back in my office in about two hours. Meet me there and we can discuss the subject of Faith." said Pastor Thomas.

"That will work out just fine. Get that: that will 'work out' just fine?"

"Dude, that was so broke." Calvin said, and they all laughed.

"Pastor T., what Calvin is trying to say is that would give us time to eat and then meet you at your office, which will be at 3 pm." said Zeteo.

"I Gotcha!" said Pastor T as she waves the 'Ok" sign at the boys.

Calvin and Zeteo went to their separate homes, and met back at Pastor Thomas's office at 2:50 pm. They greeted her as she arrived at 2:55 pm They notice that she had some bags, so they ran to help her bring in some items that she brought with her.

"Thanks, young men, I appreciate it." replied Pastor Thomas.

They walk with her as she goes up and unlocks the door to let them in.

"Please, just set those things on the executive table and have a seat." said Pastor Thomas.

As they are being seated, Pastor asked, "So, what has

sparked your interest in Faith?"

"Pastor T., we both were frustrated with where our life is at the moment." Zeteo replied as he looks at Calvin for agreement. "Don't get us wrong: we appreciate what God is doing and has done in our life. It is just that we feel that there is more that we can see occur in our lives and we want to go after all that is available."

Calvin nods his head as Zeteo continues, "And, from the lives of others that have started with little as a person and with little in personal things, we see that the quality of their life changed through the introduction of Faith into their life. Like Kenneth Hagin, who through revelation on Faith, was raised from his sick bed that doctors said he would be confined to for the duration of his life. Like Dr. I.V. Hillard, who received revelation on Faith and went from 23 members to a ministry that impacts the world; one church in multiple locations. Like Dr. Fred Price, who received revelation on Faith and built the Faith Dome in the midst of what society calls the ghetto. And multiple others who went from being broke to becoming large-scale philanthropists, like Jim Rhone and Paul J. Meyers."

Calvin jumps in, "We also see Faith working in *your* life, producing such God-glorifying demonstration. The one thing that you all have in common is the turning point that came into your lives at the crossroads and the introduction of the revelation of Faith."

Zeteo continued, "So, we want to experience change, along

with receiving all that God has for us."

Insightful Wisdom

Pastor T. pauses for a moment and then responds, "Calvin and Zeteo, it is great that this has been awakened in you. I understand that much has to do with the call on a person's life; but, it is obedience *and* Faith that have to respond to the call. It also involves hearing God's voice clearly, and then having the courage to obey His voice and carry out the instructions. Again, even that requires Faith to activate the obedience. I have learned that Faith is work, and a person of Faith is always working something forward and working vision forward. I have also come to understand that Faith is always an action term, and those that take actions in Faith with consistency as a lifestyle experience the fulfillment of The Word of God in their life." as she taps her hands, one on top of the other, on her desk. "So, I commend you both for your pursuit, and for determining and conforming your life into the image of Faith."

Zeteo asked, "So, what advice can you provide on the subject of Faith?"

As her eyes light up, Pastor T begins to share her insights on the matter of Faith. "Calvin and Zeteo, it must be understood that Faith is a process that involves the belief system. This is important for us to be aware of because our Faith is processed through our belief system. And, if it is defective, then our Faith is going to be defective. Then, once this awareness occurs, the person can go to work on their Faith with focus and purpose."

"Hmmm!" responded Calvin and Zeteo.

Pastor Thomas continues, "Also, I would share that there must be an understanding and appreciation for the Faith process to experience Faith and partake of its benefits and positive outcomes."

"But, what is a *belief system*?" Calvin asked.

"Well, let me explain it like this. A *belief system* is a set of principles or tenets that we unconsciously live by. They influence how we perceive possibilities in life. The framework of the belief system is formed by what we experience or have been told by credible others. Together they form the basis of what we say or see, as well as what we deem is right and wrong, what is true and false, what is doable or not doable, and what we see about ourselves as being qualified or not qualified to receive. Do you understand?" as she looks at the boys for agreement.

Calvin and Zeteo look as if they are getting it a little bit.

Pastor Thomas continues, "Look at it this way. Over the process of time, we develop convictions within each one of these areas that I just mentioned. Convictions are like concrete slabs in the mind that hold us in a certain way of thinking and in certain perceptions of life; and they also dictate what we see as possible for ourselves. So, if there are bad experiences and/or negative words from credible others rooted in us, it will defuse and break down our Faith – or, put another way, what we see as possible and what can muster to believe we can receive.

"Well Pastor T., how does a person overcome the convictions that have been developed through being exposure to anti-Faith developing conversations, and those who were deemed credible that have filled a person's mind with negative images about themselves?" asked Calvin.

"That is a good question and one that speaks to the life of many individuals." replied Pastor Thomas. "The journey to come out of that conditioning is going to begin with the understanding of two basic points:

The *first point* is this: Faith begins where the will of God is known and the person becomes intimately acquainted with His will.

And, the *second point* is this: Faith begins where identity is known – when we find our identity in God.

When you read through the book of Galatians, you can see that it is written with the thread of contending for identity in God by Faith.

This identity is a love identity; meaning we love Him because He first loved us. Thus, we seek revelation of and the rooting of His love for us to occur in us. This will produce a greater love for Him. (You who are reading this book, re-read Ephesians prayers in Chapters 1 and 3.)

Then, our love for and toward God must translate to Faith that we exercise by the grace of God. Get this love-truth because it is important: Faith worketh by Love. From there, become masterful in the skillful use of The Word of God. Remember, Faith is the confident belief that causes me to act per that specific spoken Word of God that also causes me to speak in agreement with the internal picture that the Word draws in me. I will speak that picture with conviction because that which is inwardly seen has become my reality."

Pastor Thomas grabs both of their hands and says, "I need you to get *that part,* young men. The inward picture that is drawn by The Word of God must become your reality; even more of a reality than what is on the outside.

"Yes ma'am." says Calvin. "We get it! The inward picture is like the revelation of something that projects an impression on the canvas of your imagination that is seen so clearly inwardly that you chase its fulfillment. It is your reality, and it becomes a truth that you have a conviction about that produces heart-felt Faith for which the person speaks Faith-filled words in agreement with it."

"That is it, young man!" said Pastor Thomas as she gives Calvin a high five. "So, lay hold on this point as well: A born-again spirit brings with it new senses that we experience as spiritual senses, an awareness of the unseen reality; all of which operate in the 5th dimension, the unseen arena. So then, Faith is spiritual material with the natural impact that dominates in both the physical and the spiritual realm."

Pastor Thomas slides the bible on the table over to the boys and says, "Look at 2 Corinthians 4:18 *While we look not at the things which are seen, but at the things which are not seen: for the things which are seen are temporal; but the things which are not seen are eternal.* We must believe, which occurs by the act of my will to trust, truly trust, and place all of my weight on a thing. It is unrestricted reliance upon a credible source that is accepted fully and trustfully. To do so, to accomplish this level of believing – which is possible through a born-again spirit – there must be a proper and healthy belief system."

Pastor Thomas pauses and tells the boys to write this down: **Spiritual Truth***: You and I will have in life what we take in Faith – believing, receiving, and claiming.*

Pastor Thomas continues, "Now, when the believer has gone all the way in – meaning that there is an abandonment of the reasoning and the use of the physical sense realm for verification – whereby the supernatural is conceivable and perceivable, and the spiritual senses are elevated in the realm of the spirit where the believer's life exists and thrives. This will enable one to walk in the integrity of The Word of God and The Law of Faith that governs that spiritual realm – The Kingdom of God. Then the supernatural is conceivable and perceivable."

Pastor Thomas goes on to say, "Gentlemen, everything is encrypted into a code inside of us, and we must study to unlock that code along with the laws that govern those codes so that we can *operate them deliberately*." Pastor Thomas pauses again, grabbing the boys' attention more intensely.

"Please don't fly past that last statement," she said, "as it has a lot of weight and juice that is to be drawn out of it. The key phrase in that last statement is *operate them deliberately*."

"Yes ma'am, I heard that. Please continue breaking this down for us." replies Zeteo.

Calvin chimes in, "We are getting it, Pastor T. Keep going."

"Good! You see, time needs to be taken to understand and operate the Law of Faith – this is called science – and it means the study of laws. The word *operate* communicates that one exercises effort deliberately; which means it is intentional and thought through, targeted, and in expectation of results."

Imagination Canvas

Pastor Thomas sits back in her chair and continues. "Young men, I want you to take good note of this point I am getting ready to make. Are you listening?"

In unison they both say, "Yes ma'am Pastor T!"

Pastor Thomas replies, "Okay, here it is: Those who master this principle of operating the Law of Faith and perform it at a biblical level, they provide the difference between those who are seeing spiritual results and those who are not. When I learn, understand, and submit to being governed by this spiritual law, coupled with patience, my life will be transformed and my life will amazingly please God.

"Pastor T, you mentioned patience. Why?" asked Zeteo.

"Patience is the main ingredient to endurance, which is what I call sustained persistence." replied Pastor Thomas.

"*Sustained Persistence*?!" exclaimed Calvin.

"Yes, *Sustained Persistence.*"

Calvin sat up on the edge of the seat and said, "Would you explain that?"

"Sure!" answered Pastor Thomas. "Sustained Persistence is the process of holding in place the image of what you are believing for – which is your inner picture – in the thinking substance of the Holy Spirit until manifestation."

"Wow! That was profound!" said Zeteo. "Would you state that one more time?"

"Sure!" answered Pastor Thomas again. "Sustained Persistence is the process of holding in place, the image of what you are believing for, which is what The Word of God or your imagination has crafted as your inner picture – holding that in the thinking substance of the Holy Spirit until manifestation. The bible states it like this:

> [36]*For ye have need of patience, that, after ye have done*

> **the will of God, ye might receive the promise.**
> [Hebrews 10:36]

and

> [12] **That ye be not slothful, but followers of them who through Faith and patience inherit the promises.** [Hebrews 6:12]

An issue occurs when the canvas of our imagination is marred."

"Wait! Wait! Wait!" exclaims Calvin. "*The canvas of our imagination*? Pastor T., you have to explain that to me. What is meant by the canvas of our imagination?"

Pastor Thomas chuckles, "I got you, and here is the understanding. Naturally, the canvas is 'a strong, coarse, unbleached cloth made from hemp, flax, cotton, or a similar yarn, used to make items such as sails and tents and as a surface for oil painting." In relationship to the canvas of our imagination, no one can physically touch a mind because it is spiritual material; yet, inside the mind, on the spiritual surface of imagination (i.e., vision and dream room) you can create images, pictures, and blueprints. Every Mozart painting began inside and was in full development on the canvas of his imagination. Then, its reality was transferred outwardly to the canvas. Every skyscraper started inside and was in full development in a blueprint on the canvas of the imagination. Then, its reality was transferred outwardly by being constructed. Every Michelangelo sculpture started inside and was in full development in the image on the canvas of the imagination. Then, its reality was transferred outwardly to manifestation. As with all creations, they are all first seen fully developed inside and then skillfully transferred outside in shape and physical appearance. However, when the canvas of the imagination is marred, meaning disfigured, through negative words, criticism, and environments that discourage possibility, or that reinforces negative self-image and self-worth, it prevents the surface of imagination from holding a picture, image, or blueprint in place long enough to become clear, real, and strong."

Zeteo asked, "So, how will a person know their imagination is marred?"

Calvin speaks up, "I think I can answer that! A marred imagination can be identified through a person's conversation. It is identified through the things they say about themselves, whether it is in affirmation of a positive self-image, or disparaging remarks about their worth, their future, or what they see as possible. I remember hearing a person say, 'I can listen to you for five minutes and tell what life will be for you in the future.'"

Zeteo chimes in, "So, a person's imagination can take them anywhere they want to go. But, a marred imagination will prevent them from seeing that there is anywhere to go."

Pastor T. replies as she applauds, "I like those two points! So, I would encourage you to go to work on the words you speak and your self-image that influences your imagination. Imag-I-Nation – it is the Image about yourself and how far you see that you can go. It is also critical in receiving and working out Faith. In these areas of self-image and imagination, I received a strong foundation from my parents. They instilled in me self-value and the possibility of doing and accomplishing whatever I set my mind and behavior to. As a result, not only I, but each of my siblings as well, have been blessed to make great strides in life, from doctors to educators. S o, I will say to anyone who will listen, you must begin with the development of a healthy self-image through finding your eternal identity in Christ Jesus. This is done by recognizing a few things. The first of which is that you are *fearfully and wonderfully made*, and you came with instructions to all that they handle you with care. Therefore, it is important to see yourself as God sees you, and that you find your identity in Him, through His Son, Jesus Christ."

Pastor Thomas has the boys look in her bible again. "Let's look at a few more scriptures to bring out these points.

[26]*And God said, Let us make man in our image, after our likeness: and let them have dominion over the fish of the sea, and over the fowl of the air, and over the cattle, and over all the earth, and over every creeping thing that creepeth upon the earth.* [Genesis 1:26]

[17]*Therefore if any man be in Christ, he is a new creature: old things are passed away; behold, all things are become new.* [2 Corinthians 5:17]
and
and ye are complete in him, which is the head of all principality and power: [Colossians 1:10-11]

Understanding these spiritual truths, and internalizing them – meaning putting them in your heart and thought process –

must become your goal. Once this goal is achieved and becomes an established principle in you, it will become the guideline for your life and the application of your belief-system. This will result in you boldly exercising the spirit of Faith. Then, the next step is to apply the spirit of Faith to where the will of God is made known, which is where the implementation of applied confident believing - Faith – begins. Once the application is practiced as a way of life, and it is coupled with the Laws of Holy Spirit – the governing power of God's Kingdom – then you will become a law-abiding citizen in the Kingdom of God where *Walking by Faith* is your way of life."

Calvin interrupts, "Pastor T., this is really good stuff!"

Zeteo chimes in, "Yeah! I have never heard this like *this* before!"

"Yes you have. You just didn't realize it was this important at the time you heard it. Let's continue looking at scripture:
> **20** *For the kingdom of God is not in word, but in power.*
> [1 Corinthians 4:20]

and

> **17** *For the kingdom of God is not meat and drink; but righteousness, and peace, and joy in the Holy Ghost.* [Romans 14:17]

Walking by Faith is something that requires an awareness

of how important it is to conduct our life by Holy Spirit relationship, strong character, and the Law of Faith. All three interwoven together are vital to our success in God, and enable us to demonstrate His way of being and doing right. To fully embrace this, one must abandon all sympathy plays, which is the constant mention of deficits and handicaps; i.e., excuses. One must also break through mental limits to open up the doorway that will enable one to produce the Faith fruit that accompanies obedience to Holy Spirit, Christ-like in one's Character, and the Spiritual Law of Faith. With this insight, we have the principles of Faith and the method of Faith that we are to exercise. We must use them to tap them to tap into the realm of Faith where the spiritual blessings are seen. The scripture calls it *"Heavenly Places."*

> *[3]Blessed be the God and Father of our Lord Jesus Christ, who hath blessed us with all spiritual blessings in heavenly places in Christ:* [Ephesians 1:3]

It will drive behavior and the correct believing attitude, which will affect the way we think, speak and conduct ourselves."

"Wow!" said Zeteo. "I can see just how much of a difference it makes when a person is governed by their senses, specifically the sense of sight, compared to a person who is governed by the Spirit of Faith operating in the spiritual realm and the eyesight of Faith."

"I know!" said Calvin. "It is like living in a different

reality without denying what is in the earth realm. The earth realm is why we need the spirit of Faith. We have to apply the *Spirit of Faith* to dominate the earth realm."

"Right!" exclaimed Pastor Thomas.

Then, the church secretary knocks on the door and lets Pastor Thomas know that her next appointment just arrived.

"Well, young men. I will have to honor my appointment. It was indeed a pleasure speaking with you today!" as she stands up to walk the boys out of her office. "I will be available next Tuesday if you should need me."

"Thanks, Pastor T." replied Zeteo. "We will treasure what you have shared! As a matter of fact, Calvin and I are going to sit down later tonight and discuss our takeaways from all that we have learned about Faith thus far. We are going to look at what Faith means, how to exercise Faith, and how to live by Faith."

"You do that, young men! Love you!" Pastor Thomas responded and she embraced each of the boys.

Calvin and Zeteo replied, "Love you too, Pastor T.!"

Calvin and Zeteo speak to the secretary and the waiting guest, and leave with such tremendous excitement about how their understanding of Faith has grown.

"Calvin, I am so excited about operating by Faith." Zeteo stated. "I is like I have gained a new lease on life."

Calvin laughs and chuckles, "I feel what you feel! And, that new lease on life is like getting another chance to do something from a different perspective."

"I am looking forward to sitting down and making a list of what we have come to understand about Faith." Zeteo continued. "We can put it in our own words."

"Sure! It is going to be amazing!" said Calvin.

"I am going to make it home, take care of a few things, and then meet you at your house after I finish." said Zeteo.

"About what time are you thinking? asked Calvin.

"At about 8 pm." Zeteo answered.

"Okay, I will see you then."

CHAPTER 8:

FAITH WORKS

Once Calvin arrives home, his father and mother ask, "Where did you go today?"

"Zeteo and I were with Pastor T. getting some of the wisdom and insight that she has." Calvin follows that up with, "She is a wonderful example of how to work the principle of Faith with consistent results."

Calvin's dad asked, "So do you think you are learning some different things related to Faith?"

"Yes sir! Zeteo and I are going to talk about the things we have learned when we get together tonight; along with how to work them into our life." Calvin says with amazement, "But mom and dad, you know what I have noticed during this process that has surprised me?"

"What is that son?" replied Calvin's mother.

"I have noticed that so many people in the church ignore Faith and the importance of its development in their life."

"What do you mean by *ignoring*?" asked Calvin's father.

"Okay. Let's do this: Reflect over the last thirty

days on the various conversations you have had with people in the church, and tell me how many of them were on the subject of Faith and how to develop Faith?"

"Well Calvin? Hum!" as Calvin's father pounders the question. "Besides you, no one."

Calvin continues, "Now, examine those same thirty days and tell me how many people came to you complaining or placing the responsibility to pray for them on your shoulders?"

Calvin's parents look silently at Calvin with concern about what he is saying.

"People do not actively pursue Faith, which is a tragedy because Faith is the core to everything we do in life. Faith is used when a business is launched, when entering college, when taking risks in investments. You name any pursuit in life, and somewhere in the mist you are going to find the use or need for Faith. "

Calvin's parents look at each other in amazement, then look back at Calvin.

Calvin continues, "The ultimate orientation of Faith I have seen in scripture is these: the God-kind of Faith, the Faith of God, and Faith toward God! Just think about it for a moment, Mom and Dad. The bible so clearly points out the importance of Faith in the Christian life." Calvin grabs the bible off the bookshelf and sits on the ottoman in front of his parents. " Let's examine the following verses of scripture together:

> *⁵Who are kept by the power of God through Faith unto salvation ready to be revealed in the last time.* [1 Peter 1:5]

This means we are shielded, preserved, and held in safety by Faith.

> *¹⁴That the blessing of Abraham might come on the Gentiles through Jesus Christ; that we might receive the promise of the Spirit through Faith.* [Galatians 3:14]

This means the Holy Spirit is received by Faith.

> *¹²That ye be not slothful, but followers of them who through Faith and patience inherit the promises.* [Hebrews 6:12]

This means the promises are received by Faith.

> *⁴Behold, his soul which is lifted up is not upright in him: but the just shall live by his Faith.* [Habakkuk 2:4]

This is why Jesus said so many times, '*thy Faith hath made the whole.*'"

Calvin's Dad interjects, "Keep going son. You're on to something!"

"Yes sir!" replied Calvin.

> "*⁶But without Faith it is impossible to please him: for he that cometh to God must believe that he is, and that he is a rewarder of them that diligently seek him.* [Hebrews 11:6]

This means Faith is the very element that is required to please God.

> *¹¹According to the eternal purpose which He*

**purposed in Christ Jesus our Lord: *12*In whom
we have boldness and access with confidence
by the Faith of Him.** [Ephesians 3:11-12]
This means Faith is how we have access to God.
**23And he that doubteth is damned if he eat,
because he eateth not of Faith: for whatsoever
is not of Faith is sin.** [Romans 14:23]
This means what is not of Faith misses the mark."

"Well, teach *me* then, Son!" exclaimed Calvin's Mom.

"Mom, where have we been and what have we been
doing?" replied Calvin with bucked eyes. "Let's just keep
looking at scriptures.
7For we walk by Faith, not by sight [2
Corinthians 5:7]
This means our behavior and conduct are to be governed by
that of Faith. And, how many times have we quoted this
verse?
**1Now, Faith, is the substance of things hoped
for, the evidence of things not seen.** [Hebrews
11:1]
This means Faith is the power of vision and expectation.

"Son, you make a very valid case, and that with scripture!"
said Calvin's father. "It appears that the key to a
productive life, and *to* walk with God, is Faith."

"Yes, Dad." said Calvin. "We need to see Faith as an
element that can be developed, strengthened, skilled, and
operated; and, that Faith is something we are required to
invest in and gain an understanding of. Just look at the

areas where Faith application is required:
- to gain that which is not yet in my possession,
- to gain that which is beyond my natural resources,
- to perform my God-given assignment,
- to experience the orchestration of God in the unseen arena, and
- to receive that which I desire and elect to believe God for that that is found in His Word, just to name a few."

"I am interested in hearing more about what else you and Zeteo have gained from your efforts." replied Calvin's father.

"That is great to hear, Dad! And, he should be calling at any time now to let me know he is on his way over here."

Faith Application

Just then, the doorbell rings. It is his cousin, Rachel, who is stopping by to say Hi; but, also because she too has something on her mind. She is in an emotional situation for which she needs prayer.

Calvin's mother and father are excited to see her, but could tell something was troubling her.

They exchange pleasantries and Calvin's mother gets straight to it. "Racheal, what is troubling you? I can see it on your face."

"Well, auntie," replied Racheal, "I have been praying about

an issue and it is not moving."

Calvin's Mom answered her, "I am sure it will move for you baby. You do believe that, right?"

"I hope so, auntie." said Racheal. "But right now, I don't see anything changing. It may be that I am being judged because of my past."

Calvin is thinking within himself, "This is just like what was shared in a previous conversation: *You can listen to a person for five minutes and tell where they are at.*" Calvin could not contain himself, "Cousin, let me ask you a question."

" Go ahead, cuz." answered Racheal reluctantly.

"Do you believe God has addressed your issue?" asked Calvin.

"I know He will, but in His own time. It is just taking too long." Racheal answered.

Calvin lets her know, "In hearing what you expressed so far, I am confident that I can assist you with this issue. I can assist by sharing a few things that will strengthen your God Kind of Faith and clear out some things that are in the way of your Faith toward God."

Rachel responds, "I am not sure what you are talking about, but I will hear what you have to say."

It is now getting late in the evening, and Calvin says, "In a few minutes, Zeteo should be calling to let me know he is on his way over. He and I have been working on a project, and we are going to sit down and stack up our takeaways from the research related to that project. The things that we are going to capture may have some concepts in them that would serve your need at the moment."

Rachael responds and says, "I am open to listening to that discussion, but what is it about?"

"Zeteo and I have been in search of a better understanding of Faith, and we have found a mentor who is gracious enough to help us in this search. We go see him tomorrow; but, before we make it to him, we wanted to collect our takeaways from what we have discovered on our own and from the homework he gave us."
Right after he said that the doorbell rang. Calvin's mother went to the door, opened it and it is Zeteo.

Right after he said that, the doorbell rang. Calvin's father went to the door, opened it and it is Zeteo.

"Hi, Mom," says Zeteo.

Calvin says to Zeteo, "I have been waiting on your call."

Zeteo chuckles and says, "By the time I would have called, I could be here. So, I just came on over." as he shrugs his shoulders. " Besides, I am ready to get this party started!"

"That's good! Me as well." says Calvin. "And it looks like it is going to be a round table. Dad, Mom, and my cousin

Rachel are going to join us!"

"Super! Mom, think we can get some shakes while we go over things?" asked Calvin.

"Already ahead of you! They are on the table now." said Calvin's mother.

They all make their way to the dining room table where shakes, appetizers, notebooks, and pens are in place. "Wow, Mom! This is what I call being on point!"

Everyone sits at the table and gets ready for the discussion.

"Now that everyone is situated, here is the first takeaway from what we discovered." says Calvin. "There is a difference between *Believe* and *Faith*. *Believe* is an act of your will to choose to accept something as truth or fact, even though there is no sense realm verification. It is a decision that I make based on a certain criterion. In John 19:20, after Jesus resurrection, Thomas gave his criterion for deciding to believe,...Except I shall see in his hands the print of the nails, and put my fingers into the prints of the nails, and thrust my hand into His side *I will not believe.* That is choice based on criterion."

"So, how is that different from Faith?" asked Rachael.

"Good question!" replied Calvin. "And the answer has been the turning point in our understanding of Faith and how it operates. Faith is the inner persuasion that something is true based on the Word of God that causes us to act on what we believe. Another way to state Faith is the spiritual state (attitude) of the heart (inner being) and mind (thinking) as of having that which is believed for and persuaded of it being received.

"What?" says Rachel. "Calvin, say that one more time but slower."

"Faith is the inner persuasion that something is true based on the Word of God, even though I have no sense realm evidence that causes us to act on what we believe. Faith is the spiritual state (attitude) of the heart (inner being) and mind (thinking) as of having that which is believed for and being fully persuaded of it being received."

"*Operation*?" exclaimed Calvin's mother.

"Yes, this is very important to working Faith." replied Calvin.

"Why?" Mom asked.

Calvin replied, "Because Faith is a law, and every law has a specific manner in which it operates. There are principles and rules that govern any given law, and when adhered to that law will produce the same results every time. But, those principles have to be executed to receive the consistent results.

So, here is another definition that I have for Faith. Faith is the inner persuasion that something is truth or fact, regardless of external conditions, it is an inner persuasion that causes you to act on what you believe. I liken it to confident believing put to action, put to work, and exercised. This speaks to the process of operation. So then, believing is the cornerstone to Faith. Take note that Jesus never said, 'oh ye of little believing,' or 'thy believing has made you whole,' or 'I haven't seen so great believing.' Those kinds of Faith acknowledgments when Jesus made them were based on an action, or lack of action, relating to an instruction or something heard. So, for me, Faith is belief put to action, and we need to see Faith as an element that can be developed, strengthened, and operated. Our success in God requires us to invest in understanding and working Faith."

"That makes so much sense!" said Rachael. "Because, in the book of James chapter 2 verse 20 it states: *[20]But wilt thou know, O vain man, that Faith without works is dead?*"

"Very good there, cuz! replied Calvin. "Now, here is the breakdown:
1. Accepting – embracing the source as credible.
2. Believing – choosing to be convinced of its truth even if there is no sense realm evidence.
3. Acting – behavior corresponding and in concert with what is believed.
4. Received – maintaining the vision or picture of it in its finished and completed state.

Because of number 4 above, it is important to know that the mind is the place where thoughts, perceptions, pictures, and images are housed. So, for the born-again believer, once salvation occurs, Holy Spirit wants us to work in compliance with Him by renewing our mind for the proper vision, image, and picture to be developed in our heart that is held in the thinking substance of Holy Spirit. This enables us to live by The Word of God and allows The Word images and pictures to be imprinted and stick in our spirit. Consider these scriptures:

> *3And be not conformed to this world: but be ye transformed by the renewing of your mind, that ye may prove what is that good, and acceptable, and perfect, will of God.* [Romans 12:3]
> *23And be renewed in the spirit of your mind;* [Ephesians 4:23]

From there, we begin to conduct ourselves by the power of that word picture and image inside of us. It becomes our substance and our evidence, as we walk by Faith – that picture and image – and not by sight – what is in appearance in the sense/physical realm. Then, along with the inner image, we also have the things in the spiritual realm that we can implant in our inner image and imagination."

"I see. Keep talking." said Racheal.

Calvin continues, "Good, cuz! Make special note of what is mentioned in Ephesians 1:3. The following rule in scripture verse applies to both the Word of God drawing – the inner picture/image and the things in the spiritual realm mentioned in Ephesians 1:3…all spiritual blessings in heavenly places in Christ – and that scripture is

¹⁸ While we look not at the things which are seen: [perceived by the natural senses], but at the things which are not seen [inner picture/image – things in the spiritual realm] for the things which are seen are temporal; but the things which are not seen are eternal. [2 Corinthians 4:18]"

Faith Comprehension

"This brings me to another one of our takeaways: Faith is a spirit, a substance and evidence that makes up the spiritual law of Faith and governs manifestation."

Calvin's father interrupts and says, "Wait! Did I hear you say Faith is a spirit?"

"Yes, Dad, it is scriptural." replied Calvin. "Faith is a spirit. It is another one of my takeaways that I now see as an aspect of the law of God."

"I hear ya. Say on, Son." replied Calvin's father.

"Ok Dad. Now, here is another definition that I have in association with the spirit of Faith (the state and attitude of confident believing that has corresponding action): The spirit of Faith is an inner boldness, confidence, and courage that has a paintbrush in hand with a readiness to paint the reality of the desired thing on the canvas of the imagination with the full persuasion of having it in possession. The scripture support for this takeaway is found in 2 Corinthians 4:13

¹³ *We, having the same spirit of Faith,*
according as it is written, I believed, and
therefore have I spoken; we also believe, and
therefore speak;

And this spirit of Faith cometh by hearing, and this hearing comes by The Word of God. It involves painting the inner image/picture, through The Word of God, on the canvas of my imagination. This is where I conceive and perceive my reality and exercise my confident believing which initiates the corresponding action."

Zeteo chimes in, "Well, another one of our takeaways is closely connected to that!"

"And, what is that? asked Rachael.

"Let me put it in context first." said Zeteo. "So, I had a struggle with how I saw myself."

"Now, what do you mean by that? asked Racheal.

"For starters, I downgraded myself, counted myself out, and deemed myself unqualified to receive anything from God." Zeteo answered. "<u>All because I saw myself as the cause of all my failures, mistakes, and negative occurrences in my life</u>. As a result, I condemned myself and saw God as wanting to keep His distance from me."

"I can relate to that!" Racheal replied. "I doubt that God is willing to do anything for me, or that I am the one He is speaking to. I see it as meant for someone else."

Zeteo responded, "I feel you, Racheal. But, here is where I got my breakthrough: when I learned my identity in Christ Jesus. I agreed with what God said in His word: I am complete in Christ. I used that verse to address every thought pattern that was contrary to that biblical truth by reminding myself of the truth of being complete in Him."

"Really?" replied Racheal.

" Now, it took a while! But, with consistency and perseverance, I was blessed to break free from those lower thoughts of self-defeating nature. And, I continue to reinforce it with such things as *Faith begins where identity in Christ and the will of God is known.* Once these were a reality in my spirit, they built confidence in believing, which will give me entrance into Faith. Without this quality of confidence, I was not approaching God boldly as the Word of God instructs us:

> *[16]Let us therefore come boldly unto the throne of grace, that we may obtain mercy, and find grace to help in time of need.* [Hebrews 4:16],

> *[11]According to the eternal purpose which he purposed in Christ Jesus our Lord: [12]In whom we have boldness and access with confidence by the Faith of him.* [Ephesians 3:11-12]

and

> *[14]And this is the confidence that we have in him, that, if we ask any thing according to his will, he heareth us: [15]And if we know that he hear us, whatsoever we ask, we know that we have the petitions that we desired of him.* [1 John 5:14-15]

"For me, Racheal, that one takeaway that I mentioned earlier was that one area that needed to be dealt with, and I will tell you why." said Calvin.

"Okay, I'm listening." said Racheal with one eyebrow raised.

"My ability to operate and appropriate all that is in Salvation, which is appropriated by Faith, requires me to clear out of my mind and spirit all blockages, barriers, and roadblocks to pure Faith. Those things cause the malfunction of my Faith toward God, by which, as a born-again believer, I am called on to live. This clearing out process is what I see as a part – and I am saying *apart*; not the total, but apart – of the crucifying process mentioned in Galatians 2:20 that also affirms that my life is to be a life of Faith:

> *^{20}I am crucified with Christ: nevertheless I live; yet not I, but Christ liveth in me: and the life which I now live in the flesh I live by the Faith of the Son of God, who loved me, and gave himself for me.* [Galatians 2:20]."

Racheal said with hesitancy, "I… think I'm beginning to see what you're saying. Don't stop talking though!" Everyone chucked as Calvin continued.

"Now, let's link that last scripture verse with two other verses to get the full picture of access and asking." Calvin said.

"Boy, this is blessing me!" said Calvin's father.

Everyone at the table shouted, "Me too!"

Calvin continued, "Now, here are the next two connecting verses for Faith toward God that reinforces access, asking, and receiving:
> *16 For God so loved the world, that he gave his only begotten Son, that whosoever believeth in him should not perish, but have everlasting life.* [John 3:16] and *32He that spared not his own Son, but delivered him up for us all, how shall he not with him also freely give us all things?* [Romans 8:32]

So now, Faith in Jesus gives us access to the fullness of God, which leads me to my next takeaway: We have access to ALL that Father God has, ALL that The Son has, and ALL that Holy Spirit reveals. Through Jesus Christ we have a right, by Faith, to enter in and claim it ALL. And, here is what I know: Father God loves me with all that He is and all that He has, and I have made that my conviction. Thus, my Faith and my Father God's become my inner Amen!"

Calvin now turning to his mother says, "I see that look on your face, Mom. You are asking, 'How and why can that be so?'"

"You got that right, Son!" replied Calvin's mother.

"Well, because it is what God has spoken! And, for sure it cannot be any other way. I can stand firm in this truth, knowing that Jesus is the author and finisher of my Faith. And, when He is in what I apply my believing to, it will come to pass. Hearing The Word of God becomes believing that becomes the spirit of Faith, the spirit of Faith becomes my inner conviction, that inner conviction speaks what is believed and acts on what is believed. Again, acts on what is believed because it is considered received. And since Faith – putting my believing to action – comes by hearing, and hearing by The Word of God, I have to act on the Word. The following truth in scripture confirms this point, the gospel will not profit me if it is not mixed with Faith, according to Hebrews 4:2

> *[2] For unto us was the gospel preached, as well as unto them: but the word preached did not profit them, not being mixed with Faith in them that heard it."*

Zeteo exclaims, "Calvin, this is really getting good and deep, my brother!"

"Yes, I know right!" replied Calvin. "This makes hearing super important! And, to this point, I make the following observation: By and large, there is a very important, but little-known truth, that needs to be respected and practiced. And that is this: Speaking The Word of God into your spirit – inner ear – must become as routine as breathing. This makes hearing important, whether it be your voice or the voice of credible others. Regarding this, Jesus gives two clear and specific warnings:

> *[18] Take heed therefore how ye hear: for whosoever hath, to him shall be given; and whosoever hath not, from him shall be taken even that which he seemeth to have.* [Luke 8:18]

and

> *24And he said unto them, Take heed what ye*
> *hear: with what measure ye mete, it shall be*
> *measured to you: and unto you that hear shall*
> *more be given.* [Mark 4:24]."

"The spirit of man is the most powerful ground to speak into." said Zeteo.

"True, Zeteo!" answered Calvin. "And, this is why the enemy fights so hard to access it. Taking another example of Jesus:

> *30 Hereafter I will not talk much with you: for*
> *the prince of this world cometh, and hath*
> *nothing in me.* [John 14:30]

The devil is to be evicted from our life and our spirit with nothing of his left in us! To accomplish this, we must have a living, abiding relationship with our eternal God and Father through Jesus Christ. Then, we must have The Word of God living and abiding inside us, which is achieved through consistent, deliberate,...I mean, intentional and deliberate effort. John 15:7 communicates the powerful results of this twofold abiding. Through it, Jesus guides us by His Spirit and the Word of God inside of us. Here is another spiritual truth about this twofold abiding: The revelation of His Word and His personality inside us produces a pure Faith and a powerful expectation for us to put to work on the earth. The inner visual of The Word of God that produces a clear, strong, and real picture within us, gives a confident force to our Faith. This confident force of Faith becomes the dynamite and creative ability of our words."

"Soooo,…" as Racheal starts to speak, but is interrupted by Zeteo.

"Wait! He's not finished yet, and I'm in the middle of a mental transformation." Zeteo blurts out.

Racheal responds, "Oh, really now!" as everyone chuckles. "Ok cuz, I think I'm starting to think a little differently. Please continue."

"Yeah, cuz." Calvin said to Rachael. "You look a little better than you did when you first came in the house!"

Calvin continues, "And, the next scripture reads
³Through Faith we understand that the worlds were framed by The Word of God, so that things which are seen were not made of things which do appear. [Hebrews 11:3]"

Zeteo bursts out, "Okay! Let me rest my spiritual brain. This is a lot to process! Allow me to go home and meditate on all this insight and revelation."

Everyone at the table agreed, "We need to meditate on all that we have discovered so far." said Calvin's mother.

So, everyone went to their 'neutral corners,' so to speak. They each began the process of meditating on The Word of God, along with the insight and revelation that was collectively received.

As Zeteo was walking home, he realized that he gained a concept and understanding of how Faith operates and how Faith is supposed to be applied. His heart became overwhelmed with emotions, and he said out loud to himself, "Now, I have to put all of this into action to experience the change that I desire!"

As soon as he stepped in the door of his home, his phone rang, "Hello!"

It is Calvin, "Hey Zeteo. I am thinking with excitement about our trip to Ira Mountain tomorrow."

"Wow!" exclaimed Zeteo. "I was thinking the same thing on the way home! Let's meet in the morning at the foot of Ira Mountain at about 8:00am tomorrow."

"Okay. But do you think he will be up that early?" asked Calvin.

"I have a feeling that early morning time with God is a part of his routine." Answered Zeteo. "And, God may even give him something for us to help wrap up our Faith mentorship development as we embark upon putting everything we have gained into operation."

"Sounds like a plan to me, my friend!" says Calvin.

So they hang up and went to bed.

REFLECTION 3

REFLECTION 3

What are your take a ways so at this point?

1.

_____
_____
_____.

2.

_____
_____
_____.

3.

_____
_____
_____.

Do you see anything that may be missing from your Faith development process that you can begin to implement?

_____
_____
_____
_____
_____
_____
_____
_____.

Is there anything that you will begin to do differently?

1.

_____

_____

_____.

2.

_____

_____

_____.

3.

_____

_____

_____.

CHAPTER 9:

FAITH INTERACTIVE

The next morning Zeteo and Calvin arrive at 7:45am with a notebook and pen, and they begin the ascent up Ira Mountain.

"Calvin, I am excited about meeting with Mr. Nootropic again!" said Zeteo as they trudge up the mountain. "And I am so glad that we are making this Faith journey together!"

"Same here, my friend! Same here." Calvin replied.

Upon reaching the place of Mr. Nootropic's abode, they find him sitting in his chair out front as though he is watching and waiting for a guest to arrive. "Good morning, young men!" said Mr. Nootropic. "I have been looking forward to your return."

They looked at each other, and simultaneously asked him "Why? For, it is we that seek a Faith mentor?"

Mr. Nootropic responds, "Yes, this is true. But, any mentor is overjoyed at the opportunity to pour into the development of the mentee."

The boys respond together, "That is true."

"Because of that, please, both of you have a seat. There are a few things that have been placed on my heart to impart into your life before you leave today." Then, Mr. Nootropic says, "It is my thought that you are going to receive some finishing touches for your Faith development that is going to elevate your life and its quality; that is, once you put the principles that you have learned and what you are going to receive this morning into practice."

Zeteo replies, "We are seated with notebook and pen, and ready to receive."

"Then, let us get started." replied Mr. Nootropic. "I want to give you this cornerstone truth that must be understood as a matter of a key element to following the Faith pattern set forth by God. That spiritual truth is this: Nothing that our God and Father made was made by accident. He was deliberate and intentional, and creation demonstrates a thoroughly thought-out approach with an intentional design that would produce specific and consistent outcomes. One example of this would be the Law of the Seed. God was intentional in the design of the seed to ensure that it consistently reproduces after its kind. He took His creative words and spoke them with an expectation of the desired results. This is a demonstration of *Deliberate Faith*."

"*Deliberate Faith*?!" interjects Calvin.

"Yes, *Deliberate Faith*." replied Mr. Nootropic. "*Deliberate Faith* is identifying with specificity what you desire to receive. It is established believing, confidence, trust, and reliance that is accompanied by corresponding actions that align with what you believe you have received. The Word of God that is rooted in deliberate faith is heard inside, which develops an inward picture of what is possible and what is in possession in the now. It is not anything I can put my finger on; but, when you experience it, you know it."

"What's that?" asked Zeteo.

"That is when you hear inwardly what you have deliberately set your Faith for." replied Mr. Nootropic, and he continues, "So then, Faith comes by hearing – receiving an inner picture of what's possible that becomes what is received in possession. That inner picture is so clear, so strong, so intense, so sincere and so real until it brings a speaking voice within. A voice you hear speaks inside that affirms the existence and the possession of the thing you are confidently believing for. This accompanying voice can also be called a knowing."

Mr. Nootropic takes a breather. Calvin and Zeteo listen attentively for the next Faith principle that he prepares to share. They ready their pen and notebook as Mr. Nootropic shares the next point.

Mr. Nootropic continues, "There is another concept that is in direct correlation to this truth and reinforces Faith for a consistent outcome. We must also be intentional about eliminating everything that could derail Faith, or misalign us regarding what is required to achieve ambitious Faith projects. Faith involves visually and emotionally living in the existence of the thing one is in confidently believing Faith for. The desired results get frustrated by obstacles and opposition to the concept of Faith. We *receive* a paradigm shift when we have unobstructed faith, which is working inwardly, mentally, and verbally until it is physically materialized. And, please keep this spiritual truth in sight: all believing has an object, a Word of Truth coupled with a practiced principle, along with correlating and corresponding actions. Our objective is to work Faith. To work Faith, we must have an understanding of Faith's structure, Faith's function, and Faith's operation. A component of Faith's structure is the spirit of Faith, which is the mental position and spiritual attitude, disposition, and spiritual condition for actionable belief."

"That was a mouth full! said Calvin.

"I understand. So let me state it again. A component of Faith's structure is the spirit of Faith, which is the mental position and spiritual attitude, disposition, and spiritual condition for actionable belief."

"Yes, I hear it." said Calvin. "I'm just trying to wrap my head around it!"

"I understand." Mr. Nootropic affirms and continues. "Faith's function has an authoritative demand. It is believing and receiving with the understanding of one's right to have it. Faith's operation is hearing, speaking, and confirming confident believing is alive through echoing the in-voice of your knower and attaching actionable behavior to it. It is an attitude of assurance and confidence that is a state of being. Trust with confident belief brings assurance of the desired results. Faith fights discouragement. It is employing resistance against disappointment in the imagined appearance of loss. Faith enables one to stay above the line of negative statements and outlooks. The Word of Faith is inner revelation spoken outwardly. It is an element and an attribute, as well as a state of mind and spirit. Remember that we, being made in the image and likeness of God, are designed with the capacity, the functionality, and the propensity for having and operating by Faith. God operates by Faith; it is His essence. So, when we operate by Faith, it reflects Him. It is taking what we have been designed and engineered with, and directing it in belief in Him to receive. We are to master the quality of this Faith in a way that it will please Him that has made us. So then, Faith is not a wish list."

Zeteo interrupts, "Faith is not a wish list. That's good!"

"Indeed it is not." replied Mr. Nootropic. "Faith is spiritual material with power in the born-again spirit, which we can grow. So, sow your Faith to ***Grow*** your Faith."

"Sow your Faith to ***Grow*** your Faith. I caught that" said Calvin."

"Yes!" answered Mr. Nootropic. "I believe you can have anything God wants you to have in life by elevating your confident belief, trust, and reliance on God and The Word of God. To this point, I have noticed in scripture that, for every principle, prophecy, and promise, there is a Faith process to bring it to pass; a strategic plan received for execution."

Here's a thought that Mr. Nootropic pointed out for the boys to write down: the born-again believer in Jesus Christ who is not studying Faith, is like a doctor not studying medical terminology and medicine, or a lawyer not studying law. The believer must study Faith because it is the way of the Christian life.

Mr. Nootropic continues, "The book of Romans states '*The just shall live by Faith.*' To activate this process of living by Faith, intentional effort is required. My Faith must become active in all matters for which I believe. It is to become emotional in my experience. Once it becomes an emotional sensation of one being in the possession of it, the person believing gravitates toward the object, and the object gravitates toward the person. It is then worked into manifestation through corresponding Faith actions and the orchestrating of events and people needed to bring it to pass. When it comes to operating in Faith, it is not wacky or weird, neither is it the denial of reality; but rather, the acknowledgment of what the word of God says. It is the choice to side with what God says, and to make a statement in agreement with His statement about any matter a person has set themselves to believe for. The statement, along with the desire, is qualified by the Word of God."

Mr. Nootropic tells the boys to write this down: Desire, wholly given over to that which has been qualified by The Word of God, which is registered and resolved in one's heart, produces a conviction that is translated into commitment. Where there is the commitment to the object of Faith there is a strong grip on receiving.

Diving Deep

Mr. Nootropic continues, "We are to verbally call what is emotionally experienced in the internal, unseen realm into manifestation in the external realm. Note the following verses as an affirmation of the truth to this principle:

- I Corinthians 2:9-14
- Romans 4:17
- II Corinthians 4:13
- In John 20:28"

"Be not Faithless but believing, according to John 20:28. Believing is actively living in the unseen and calling it so as an act of your will. It is accepting it as true without sense realm evidence. Jesus was telling Thomas to live that way; not just for that moment, but continually. Live and believe based on The Word of The Lord – His record of the unseen. John 15:7 – what you will – vividly imagined and considered received and emotionally experienced. Lock into it with laser-focused and needle threading concentration. **The just shall live by Faith – by** the method of Faith, by the system of Faith, and by the principle of Faith. It is not living by *a wish*, not living by *a want,* nor is it living by a *'should I have it.'* It is a process that leads to a place where one has wholly given over to it as having and owning it. It is where having the believed thing becomes a must; and when that place of must is reached, this is when one will have it. Again, it is vividly imaging, which would mean that in the unseen realm I live as though having already received it. This is operating by Faith."

CHAPTER 10:

MR. NOOTROPIC'S DISSERTATION ON FAITH

Mr. Nootropic seems to switch into professor mode as he continues with his dissertation on Faith.

*Please note: All "**Special Note**" sections throughout this dissertation are items that Mr. Nootropic had the boys write on their paper.*

"When it comes to operating by Faith, we must assume the responsibility for going into the Spirit and visiting what we are believing for and walking it out as though it is so. Experiencing what we believe for in our imagination and becoming emotionally rooted and grounded in it (whatever I am believing for) and coming back and calling them into the physical realm is the operation of Faith. When what you are believing for is emotionally experienced, it becomes a reality in you that is established in your spirit and mind, which will make it yours to believe and receive. This part of the process has to be protected from anything that would generate doubt, cause questions, or produce uncertainty. These types of interferences can occur when we try to rush the process. It needs to be understood that the Faith process must go through its cycle just like a seed that is planted. The farmer does not rush the harvest. Why? Because he knows it must go through its cycle. Once this Faith cycle is understood, it will reinforce the discipline and cooperation necessary to see the Faith operation through to manifestation. Discipline holds one accountable to do what one knows is supposed to be done, how it is supposed to be done, and when it needs to be done. Discipline is the ability to tell yourself *'No'*, and the might to override the *'I don't feel like it'* and the *'not now's.'* When this is done long enough until it becomes consistent, it creates a groove called *conditioning and habit*, and the habit becomes a lifestyle.

God's spiritual force of the intellectual thinking substance of Holy Spirit is working on our behalf. And he knows the mind of God because He is the Spirit of God. This means He knows the will of God toward us and The Word He wants for us. He works to guide our prayers and streamline them for the fulfillment of that word spoken for our life. It is a process that is conducted by the Spiritual operation of Faith found in Mark 11:24."

"The Faith cycle looks like this:

- *Whatsoever thing*... II Peter 1:3-4; 1st Corinthians 2:9-14
- *You desire*... Point, aim, target your intention, focus and emotions to have, being specific about it Matthew 4:6.
- *When you pray*...Ask and it... James 1:5
- *Believe you receive them*...Rom 8:32; James 1:6; Rom 4:17, 21
- **And you shall have them**...Ask and receive 1st John 3:18-22"

"Obedience accompanies and confirms that you believed you received, Romans 4:17; Matthew chapters 7 – 9; James 2:22-26."

Special Note: The desire for it precedes asking, and understanding precedes receiving, and receiving precedes the transfer from the spiritual realm into the natural realm.

Spiritual Truths to Note:
- *We have His righteousness with His permission to use it.*
- *We reign in life through Christ Jesus*
- *For as He is, so are we on the earth*
- *Walk as He walked*
- *Your belief is controlled by your hearing*
- *Your self-image is connected to your believer*
- *Your believer is fed by your seeing what is perceived and comprehended physical as reality.*

"Everything from creation involved God speaking and creation hearing. Understand this: What you inwardly visualize must become authentic to you. In like manner, everything done in the Kingdom through the church has been via a man or woman of God hearing God, obeying God, and believing in God to show up through the element of Faith. Also understand, we set things in motion even though the material realm has not yet manifested it. Obeying this principle and practicing it will improve the quality of your life on purpose as it sets things in the unseen realm into motion."

Calvin and Zeteo, when what's in God, by way of Word image, gets in you and becomes reflected, represented, and mirrored inside of you, then it becomes authentic (meaning it is so clear, so strong, so intense, so sincere and so real that it becomes uncomfortable to live outside of that picture) because it becomes truth to you. This is what God wants us to do as revealed in Psalms 1:1-3; Joshua 1:8-9; 1 Timothy 4:13-15. Believing is fully embracing and being convinced of its existence and truth as an act of your will. Things start happening when I believe and start speaking it according to 2 Corinthians 4:13. When believing is complete – fully formed in me – then agreement occurs unconsciously as a secret code of Faith which influences corresponding behavior. Thus, a deeper truth of believing is this: Even though it is an act of my will to accept as truth, and even though there is no sense realm evidence, once complete and formed in me, which causes my believing capacity to expand. It is still unconsciously occurring because it moves from a conscious will to an unconscious feeling and knowing. This is when the process enters the belief system. A healthy belief system is the basis of Faith.

Special Note: *God, our Father and Lord, has a covenant love for us. Job 5:4-7 communicates that His covenant love cannot be topped, nor can anyone win against those whom His covenant love is targeted, according to Deuteronomy 4:5-7, 1 John 2:3-5, and Revelation1:5-6. Perfect love casts out fear according to John 15:7, 1 John2:3-5, 1 John 3:23-24, and 1 John 4:18.*

Another principle to lock in is this: Faith and believing, in a biblical sense, are covenant terms. The covenant of God is superior in authority and power, and is above anything else, and rules above anything else. The covenant of God possesses the ability, potency, authority, and greatness to raise anyone and move anyone out of anything; break the hold of anything, and place anyone in the provisions of heaven and the provisions of earth. Receiving revelation of God's love for us serves to build a healthy belief system.

Our prayer should be: *Lord give me a healthy belief system to strengthen my belief and build my capacity to believe because I need to believe it exists for me and is received by me. I will know things are happening inside me when I start speaking it, whatever it is I am believing for!*"

Special Note: *Believing is accepting the truth of it being in existence, being doable, and it being receivable. Faith then is reaching for it as though you own it in possession. Believing will move from a conscious act of my will to a subconscious feeling.*

"Calvin and Zeteo here a few questions for you to ponder and answer:
- What is your believer occupied with right now? If it's nothing, then give it something.
- What is your believer threading the needle on? If nothing, then give it something."

Special Note: *We can only walk out the discipline our belief system ingests, accepts, and holds as truth. When you receive understanding and get revelation – which comes with registering and being rooted in the truth – the inner image that believing and receiving produces becomes an inner witness.*

Mr. Nootropic continues, "Integrity comes from God: give your word and keep your word. Be truthful and walk a straight line doing what is right. There is a location in your believing mindset that consists of a set place – a believing mindset – an existing realization that there is something you're settled on. It is an assurance occurring in the belief world that concludes that it is and is to be; that it is so, and it is received."

Special Note:
- *Jesus Christ is our way into the forgiveness of God*
- *Jesus Christ is our way into the salvation of God*
- *Jesus Christ is our way into the inheritance of God*
- *Jesus Christ is our way into the power of God*

Mr. Nootropic picks up again, "It is also discovered that the Faith experience is based on the level of commitment one makes to God, and is reflected on the level of investment that you have made in your relationship with God. It could be stated in the following way: How far into God are you? How deeply are you rooted in God? How strong are you in His power and the power of His Spirit? When you reach the *all-in* level of commitment, then the experience produces a reality persuasion. When everything of God is counted real and sought out with conviction of its existence, and entered by action, believing and speaking without hesitation, reservation, or intimidation, then manifestation will occur.

Faith Necessities

'Only Believe…' The devil can't do anything to erase your

Faith if your mind and your spirit do not buy into what he says. Remember, believing is based on choice, the will to accept as truth.

Special Note: What are your criteria for believing? What must be in place before you decide to believe it?

Understand this: Our belief system dictates our criterion for setting our will to believe.

Consider this: The power of God in the finished work in Christ Jesus on the cross transcends sickness and disease with healing. The power of God in the finished work in Christ Jesus on the cross transcends the enemy's attack with victory. The power of God in the finished work in Christ Jesus on the cross transcends lack and poverty with provisions, prosperity, and increase.

The flow of abundance, wealth, and riches is a part of our inheritance. Our spiritual blessings are in the inheritance we received from Jesus Christ. We have an inheritance amongst them that is sanctified. Anything in the way of a need that comes up, or anything I can ask for, is already there in my inheritance. How could that be so? Because He already knew what I would have need of, and nothing about me has caught God off guard. He already surveyed my life before I was formed; so, anything I could have imagined or encountered, Father God already calculated the scenario, the mistake, and the need and made provision. So, now we can say, according to Philippians 4:19 and Ephesians 3:20, that our needs are met exceeding and abundantly above all that we can ask or think.

Special Note: *Never be intimidated about saying what you are believing for and what believing is pushing out. Just meditate on the following verses and keep moving forward:*
- *John 16:23*
- *James 1:1-7*
- *1 John 5:13-15*
- *Philippians 4:6-8*
- *Matt 6:9-11*
- *Duet 4:7-8*
- *Duet 8:18*
- *Mark 9:23*

Believing also means accepting and understand the spiritual operation of God and embracing it by choice. So, to enforce this, there must be:

· A mindset for coming out on top
· A strategy for coming out on top, and
· A discipline to stay on top.

God has Faith as His essence and He is Omni-Present – present everywhere at the same time, which means: He saturates the atmosphere; thus, the atmosphere is programmed and pre-engineered to respond to Faith. In Him is our inheritance. Everything we will ever need is in Him, and it is in Him that we live move and have our being. The atmosphere, His presence, is responsive to Faith; thus, without Faith, it is impossible to please Him. His presence duplicates and produces what is held in it. So, know that Faith is reinforced by patience. Thus, Faith and patience hold in place in thinking substance (The Presence of God) what has been imaged inside of us. Like hands, *faith* sets it in place (the thinking substance of Holy Spirit) what is believed for and holds it until the thing imaged in us is formed and brought forth until duplication occurs. He is the substance we prophesy and speak into for voice printing the object of our Faith, which pulls out the thing that is in God, understanding that the atmosphere is charged with His presence. Always remember you are the benefactor of all that God has done in Christ on the cross of Calvary and His resurrection from the dead. He gives unto us out of Himself and He gathers His resources onto us out of Himself. All things pertaining to life and godliness that have been given unto us have been reserved in heaven in spiritual blessings, formed and packaged in a Word of Promise, awaiting the Faith process that will withdraw that which has been freely given unto us through Jesus Christ. Reference Ephesians 1:3, 2 Peter 1:3-4, Romans 8:32, James 1:6-7, Mark 2:23, James 4:1-3, Joshua 1:8-9, 1 John 3:22, Deuteronomy 4:5-8, 1 John 3:3, and 1 John 3:23.

Special Note: *The Faith process is a law like gravity, gravity is invisible to the eye, but it is real in how it operates, and Faith, like gravity, is real and in operation always.*

Faith Communication

"I want to restate this again! God has Faith as His essence, and He is Omni-present – everywhere present at the same time; meaning He saturates the atmosphere. Thus, the atmosphere is programmed and pre-engineered to respond to Faith; and without it, it is impossible to please God –

retrieve out of the atmosphere, the spiritual realm of thinking substance, what you say and voice imprint.

As you operate in this level of Faith, it takes on the persona of:
- My Faith has taken authority over the object of Faith
- My Faith has received it
- My Faith takes hold of it and has it
- My Faith sees it and seizes it, and
- My Faith calls for it.

Faith is our vehicle of communication. It communicates, with a strong affirmation, that God is who He says He is, and that He will do what He said He would do. Faith is also the act of holding on to the Word of God that is released, and then giving voice to it, whether it is His written or Rhema Word. It is prophesied into the atmosphere, the spiritual realm, and it speaks to the truth and essence of who He is, His Omnipresence, and His Spiritual thinking substance. That Word spoken creates an image in us and thinking substance knowing it is the Spirit mind of God. Again, I state: Faith and patience hold the image created by the Word of God in thinking substance until the image is formed clearly, and with strength, in the believer's spirit. This image takes on words when we pray. Thus, we pray out the image that is inside us. When we pray it out, God hears us with His Spiritual ear; so, we do not have to be in any physical proximity to be heard. We need only to give him confident believing (Faith). Again, to believe is to place a credit on what God says. What God has said in Psalms 145:17-

18 settles the truth of God hearing us:

> **The Lord is righteous in all His ways and holy
> in all His works. The Lord is nigh unto all
> them that call upon Him, to all that call upon
> Him in truth.**

So, the thing that needs to occur is this: Hear what God says and speak what God speaks. Faith is a spiritual muscle that requires exercise to be developed. Isaiah 46:4; 48:2-3 states that God has everything for us, all things that pertain to life and godliness. All of it is in Him and He has made the law of Faith for pulling it out of Him, and for bringing it through the realm of The Spirit into manifestation in the natural realm. We make a withdrawal from our inheritance account through the Faith process. And I do so in His name, Jehovah Jireh, the Lord who is God that sees my need afar off, who makes available total provision and continual supply. Romans 8:32; Lev 25:21-22. This truth rests in the revelation that The Lord is God and He is our provider. Once it locks into the mind that our Father is a wonderful provider with unlimited resources, unconditional love, and almighty power, it makes it easier to believe and to have Faith. My Faith is then rooted in confidence and trust in God, His ability, and the integrity of His love for me. I am made able to stand strong in His Word and believe His willingness to exercise His power of provision on my behalf.

Special Note: *One must bind the enemy that is against the increase and cast all resistance to increase out of the mind. The Lord, who is God, can do anything He wants.*

Why wouldn't He do this for you? He solved the sin issue when God was in Christ reconciling the world back unto Himself on the Cross of Calvary. The Lord, who has abundantly more beyond what I need, why wouldn't He give to me what I want and need? His Word says no good thing will He withhold from them who walk upright. Some laws are put in place by God for man to operate on the earth. God pulled these laws out of Himself for our use on the road to success and victory. It is the process of being made in His image and likeness. Because of the laws that are in Him, He uses them to override the 3rd dimension laws.

As stated before, here is what that looks like:
- I see it occurring on the inner canvas of my imagination
- I believe I have received
- My inner capacity level rises to what I see inside
- I see it as already occurring
- I lay claim to it and envision living it.

How do we affect our situation, issue, or circumstance? What we can do about it is only limited by the development, direction, and implementation of one's Faith. One's imagination, drive, actions, behavior, and decisions draw on God's unlimited resources.

Consider this: God could have left us in what we were tangled up in, and left us without Him in our lives; but, He didn't. He brought us out of those things to be God to us. Leviticus 22:31-33. This is a Faith deal – Faith is the by-product of knowing who you are, and who you are is found in God.

It must be locked in that you are born of His seed. When it is realized and conceptualized in one's spirit, it brings restoration, reconciliation, and realization of your right standing and your right relationship with God. This assures you that you have uninhibited access to God, and it is meant to empower you with boldness and with confidence.

Special Note: *Blessed means being spoken over by God for quality life and success. God does not have a 'not possible' clause or mindset. God does not have a negative detracting 'but and if' vocabulary. God has a positive and elevating 'but and if' vocabulary.*

Don't complain about not having enough money, don't complain about people asking you for money, and don't complain about those who have money. Don't try and download God into your 2X2 box thinking.

The things that ought to be clear, strong, and heartfelt are these:

- The Fatherhood of God
- The want to do of God that He has already worked out and that is found in The Word of God
- The already in me factor
- The I Received, I know, and I see

Special Note: *the verses below support these truths: Isaiah 63:16; Isaiah 56:4-5; Isaiah 57:13; Isaiah 43:10-13; Isaiah 64:4; 1st Corinthians 2:9-11; Isaiah 64:8*

Faith Platform

"Belief is the platform from which Faith is launched.

Faith never states what cannot be done, Faith awaits a process, a plan of action, and/or revelation of resources while remaining in a *'believe I receive state of mind.'*
A heart that is in a constant state of belief, and that understands the ability of God and His Faith process will see consistent results. For it is this kind of heart that embraces God's will, His willingness, and His commitment to our best outcomes. In this type of heart, any seed of The Word of God sown will produce fruit. Again, Faith is also a byproduct of knowing who you are, and that is found in God-identity. From this foundation, one can work the Faith process. W hat is the Faith process? The Faith process is a strategy and business model that blueprints the method and directions to be carried out to receive what one is believing for. God needs *us* to work His process.
When we set Faith objectives, then the objectives must be formed clearly and strongly on the inside of our hearts. What makes this aspect so important is that, once it is in place, there is no looking back.

> *My little children, of whom I travail in birth*
> *again until Christ be formed in you.* [Galatians
> 4:19]

This is a powerful truth and principle, and here is the application: We must earnestly travail in labor for what we are believing, that it **comes** to be formed in us. God wants us to be confident in Him. This involves understanding His provisional love – Romans 8:32 – and <u>exercising Faith at the same level of His love</u>. This will empower us to believe with authority. Being fully persuaded we received by asking according to His will is what He has said and says to us. Faith is becoming one with the Word of God. Faith is the person of the *is* of God that produces boldness. Again, as we grow in Faith, there are three elements of the realm of God for us to be aware of:

- The Name of Jesus is the Law of the Kingdom of God.
- God's Holy Spirit is the Power of the Kingdom of God.
- The Word of God is the rules of the Kingdom of God."

Special Note: *Dreams, visions, and images infused with Faith, have enough power to rearrange and realign environments and events.*

"All that is being revealed and understood must be meditated on and visualized so that it sinks deep in one's spirit and becomes living, breathing reality and truth. This will cast an inward vision of it as being accomplished, finished, and completed. All this equals a state. The whole process is what pro and champion athletes do all the time. I am not sure why it is thought strange when it comes to believing God in His Word. It is simply the process, the dream, the desire, the vision, and the image crafted by The Word of God (imagination and picture), and the elements of Faith at work to produce their fulfillment. Another avenue for this to occur is praying in The Holy Ghost, in one's heavenly language, which will serve to download assignments into one's heart to become an inward image and picture. It then becomes a truth and reality vision, which is to be spoken out of your mouth into the atmosphere to be worked by The Holy Ghost."

Convicted Faith

"The Lord wants the believer to see and heed Him. He causes the believer to see the success picture; then, it is up to the believer to develop the picture and walk it out. And, when He provides that picture and image inside of the believer, He is enlarging the capacity of the believer to believe Him. All that is contained inside the believer He will bring to pass; that is *God's* part. The believer is responsible and accountable to keep building and developing his or her Faith. A good acronym for Faith is **F**-ocus, **A**-nticipate, **I**-ntimate, **T**-ruth, **H**-aving it in possession. Faith is an incubator; and, when a seed is planted inside the incubator of Faith, it germinates and produces the manifestation and fruit. We want to create ground for Faith that is so fertile that a meditated thought, vision, image, dream, desire, or word placed in it comes forth with strength. A mind and heart that is Faith conditioned are conducive for the production and reproduction of what the Word of God promises."

Mr. Nootropic leans in and says, "Calvin and Zeteo, what has been examined are Faith principles, processes, and positions, all of which can be learned, revealed and understood until Faith becomes where a person lives. Faith and Faith actions will align with what the scriptures say, and that is *'the just shall live by their Faith.'* In this state of Confident believing (Faith), there will be the development of what could be called *Faith Sight.* *Faith Sight* is seeing it as done, doable, and visualized as so. Faith is also the alignment of the emotions, the mind, and the spirit of a believer with desire, want, energy, expectation, and conversation about a targeted outcome, vision, or image. The spiritual state that scripture indicates God wants the believer to live in is a consciousness of *convicted* Faith. Convicted Faith is settling on something being so, something as though it has already occurred, and as though it is already in one's possession. This requires an exit from the senses and an entrance into the spiritual awareness of the evidence of things not seen. We wake up in the sensual and thus must make a shift of our focus. Walk in the Spirit because in Him there is no limit. Know that The Holy Ghost is not held to any limit. Prayer is the first form and indication of dependence because prayer is dependent on God. It is the process of ***...looking unto Jesus the author and finisher of my Faith***. It is the action of learning to keep your eyes on Jesus and to keep His promises in front of you. It must be held in mind that The Lord God's Word is His bond, and that to be in Faith is to be one with and in agreement with God and His Word. It is being fused, producing an assurance that evolves into a reality. It is a state where you don't see yourself separated from what you're in Faith for, according to Hebrew 4:2 and John 15:7. Your season changes every time you use your Faith.

What are you releasing into the atmosphere that you can put a demand upon your Faith for?

When that is in place, it is equal to a connection with Jesus that happens thru confidence in Jesus – who He is, and what He has accomplished. His anointing is attracted to this connection, and His anointing carries with it unlimited power, unlimited wisdom, unlimited ability, and unlimited intelligence to which the believer's Faith is linked. Thus, Holy Spirit and Faith are at work for us when this is done. The believer's Faith is released from the resurrection power of The Lord Jesus Christ, which is a seat authority. It can be seen this way: Faith has a grip that lays hold on the object and will not let go until the object is received. It is equivalent to an eye being locked on it, a heart being locked on it, the expectation being locked on it, and focus being locked on it, as well as emotions being locked on it. This causes our behavior to be locked on it – it is a total giving over to it that is non-negotiable. ***The law of the Spirit and life in Christ Jesus has made me free from the law of sin and death.*** Every law has an endorsement and spiritual enforcement behind it. Because Faith is a heavenly law, all of the Kingdom of Heaven is behind it. Plus, since the Spirit of Faith is intelligent, Faith must have an objective and a target that heaven can back. The establishing of an objective and a target will occur unconsciously or consciously. It can be something that you initiate, or God can be the initiator. It can also be something your environment or a person or people initiates and assign to you, which may not be beneficial to you. The point is, it is going to occur. Since it is going to occur, why not be the one to direct it and control it. It is according to the development of your spirit as it relates to the projection of your Faith that gives root to our Faith. So then, Faith is not a strain; it is peaceful because it is a Faith state.

Faith Laws

Knowing the will of God and being in the will of God is the

entrance into this caliber of Faith that places the believer in the state of peace. Your reason for the working of your Faith is contained in the desired expectation. And, the object and target must be strong enough to lift the believer into this Faith state where there is no straining but simply Faith-ing. Since everything occurs on the inside in direct relationship to the inner knower, then one has to ensure that he or she de-clutters everything from around their knower so that it does not block or distort what one is hearing and perceiving and interpreting for the knower. Faith is an irrevocable *Yes* that prevents you from looking back and becoming double-minded. It shuts out every doubt-producing voice. Faith is spiritual material and power that impacts every realm. It is the nature of The Living Word of God. The Living Word is to be in the believer's mouth for life (creative power). It is the power of the tongue, and they that love it (work it, put it to work) shall eat the fruit thereof. There is no doubt because it is the design of the seed to reproduce after its kind. Faith agitates, activates, duplicates, and reproduces the image after its kind when it is mixed with the Word of God. This is a matter of non-negotiable law that God has already set in motion.

Calvin and Zeteo, here are a couple of laws that govern Faith:

- The Law of speaking authority- being made in the image and likeness of God

  I have speaking authority with God to ask of Him and to exercise dominion in the earth.

- The Law of Meditation – it drinks up the word of God; it muses it until it becomes an image and

- vision in the inward parts that is lived, speaks, and is spoken out

There is a reality area in us; when the image and picture reach that area, it becomes a knowing.

- The Law of desire.
- The Law of asking – it describes the characteristics and principles of the operation of Faith

What makes it? What are the components?

- The Law of self-Identity – a guide to healthy self-esteem that empowers one to see themselves in light of their identity in Christ Jesus; to celebrate their uniqueness, locate their element and watch their genius come alive
- The Law of Faith flows through peace. It works by love and an intimate connection that receives
- strength from God to build up others, and strength to strengthen them.

When these Laws just mentioned are in full maturity, together they become a Faith Power that pulls the believer toward the presence and materialization of its object. Then, one can move to turn the Will (desire and mind of Faith) to become Faith-results-oriented. Faith has a personality; and, the more focused you are about what you are aiming at the more productive Faith will be for you. Faith is a living force and has the will of desire, the will of definiteness of purpose, and the will of productivity. Faith is a spirit and has the personality of confidence, strong-ness, determination, perseverance, and boldness, with the ability to produce beyond temporal situations. Faith is an element that possesses decisiveness with par-excellent work ethics. Faith is a laser lock that has the authority to summon and draw all needed resources to accomplish its outlined diagram.

THE CONCLUSION

Mr. Nootropic continues with another **Special Note** for the boys to write down.

Special Note: *In order for Faith to work, there must be a Faith consciousness. And, consciousness of Faith's Faithfulness will produce confidence in its operation. Faith orchestrates and organizes its aim to happen.*

Mr. Nootropic ends his conversation and begins to gather his things. Zeteo and Calvin sit with several pages of notes and eyes filled with water as Mr. Nootropic wraps things up and begins to say his farewell.

Calvin asks, "So, this is the *conclusion*?" as he and Zeteo stood and watched Mr. Nootropic walking away to go into his abode.

"The conclusion is now in *your* hands." replied Mr. Nootropic. "How the *conclusion* is written is determined by how you live your life from this day forward. Will you start applying what you have learned, with the proven biblical principles, and change the quality of your life? Or, will the pages of notes that you have written be all that you have to show for your time spent with me?" as Mr. Nootropic raises his eyebrows and looks at the boys. "Here is what I know for sure!" Mr. Nootropic stands inside the door to his abode. "If you apply the Faith principles that you have discovered and learned,…," Mr. Nootropic pauses.

The boys look intensely at Mr. Nootropic and say simultaneously, "Yes, Mr. Nootropic?"

"I will see you at the top!" Mr. Nootropic leans in toward the boys and says his final word, "SHALOM!" and closes his door.

APPENDIX A

LITERAL CONVERSATIONS

Appendix A
Literal Conversations

<u>Convo 1</u>

"**Hey, Jasmine**! Would you like to hear your dad's definition of Faith?"

Jasmine's replies, "Sure dad." in a ho hum tone of voice.

"Okay, here it goes! It captures all the elements of the Faith process and the Faith Structure along with the definition: Faith is the attitude (spirit) and disposition of believing something is so, in presentence, based on the inner image/picture drawn by The Word of God (Logos or Rhema), by a dream, by a vision, or by desire that is so sincere, so clear, so strong, so real, and so intense that it cases massive action in confirmation and alignment with and in the pursuit of what is seen in that inner image/picture even when there is no sense realm evidence. It changes the way you think, speak, and act.

Jasmine retorts with an unimpressed look, "Daddy, would you like to hear *myyy* definition of Faith?"

"Yes!" I replied, excited that I have her engaged in the conversation.

"Well, Daddy. My definition of Faith is this: Belief behind an action that receives that the outcome is going to be what is wanted.

"My reply to that is, well just drop the mic, why don't ya!"

151

<u>Convo 2</u>

"Hey Daddy! What are working on?" asked Victoria.

"**Hey Victoria**! I am preparing the logistics for the Faith workshop, pulling together the lesson plan for my topic, and taking care of a few things for my job. All of them together have me going."

Victoria energetically and forcefully replied, "Power through, Dad! Power through!"

"Thank you, Victoria! "I will draw on those words anytime I feel overwhelmed."

Convo 3

"**Hey Dominique**, my number one son! How are you doing?"

"Doing good, Dad." replied Dominique with great confidence. "Dad, have I told you that I am proud of you?"

"Thanks, Son! That means a lot!"

Dominique continued, "I watch you go after your dreams, the preparation you put in, and your positive confessions. Now you are living your dream: You travel as a speaker and trainer, and you are blessing people's lives in the process. Proud of you, Pops!"

"Well, Thanks Dominique!"

REFERENCES

REFERENCES

Galileo Galilei, the Italian natural philosopher, astronomer, and mathematician. Google.com

Apostle I.V. Hilliard various recorded Faith messages

Mike Murdock's teachings on Faith (Google.com)

Webster's Dictionary

World Education Services Faith lessons (Google.com)

GLOSSARY

GLOSSARY

Believe – the act of your will to accept as fact even though you have no sense realm evidence

Canvas – a strong, coarse unbleached cloth made from hemp, flax, cotton, or a similar yarn, used to make items such as sails and tents and as a surface for oil painting

Electromagnetic Fields – a combination of invisible electric and magnetic fields of force

Faith – the inner persuasion that something is true or fact based on the Word of God that causes you to act on what you believe

Nootropic – Greek for *bend or turn the mind toward*

Sarkikós – *doubt*

Zeteo – Greek for *strive after*